Joy—it's the one ... y we describe our relationships, sea... oy also seems the most difficult to ... ief, or loss. In *The Joy Switch*, Chris ... l understanding of how our brain pro... to not only restore joy but thrive in jo, ...ia, broken relationships, or significant loss, *The Joy Switch* will offer you concrete steps to enhance and sustain a disciplined practice of joy in your daily life.

DEBORAH GORTON, PHD
Psychologist, professor, and author of *Embracing Uncomfortable: Facing Our Fears While Pursuing Our Purpose*

Everybody wants to experience joy. But it often eludes us. Coursey blends brain insight with practical wisdom to show you how you can more consistently experience joy. He deftly weaves colorful life stories into how he encourages the reader to engage their "joy switch." I recommend *The Joy Switch* to anyone who wants greater satisfaction in their relationships with people and with God.

DR. CHARLES STONE
Lead Pastor at West Park Church in London, Ontario, Canada; author of six books, including *Holy Noticing: The Bible, Your Brain, and the Mindful Space between Moments*

Politics, money, and religion—why are there topics and people we just cannot talk about? How does family love turn into shouting, silence, hurt feelings, and distance? *The Joy Switch* explains the clear mechanism in the brain that few people understand but we all see. You know you already need to know this!

JIM WILDER, PHD
Author and international speaker on the neuroscience of trauma recovery and prevention

In *The Joy Switch*, Chris Coursey presents a treasure trove of information. What makes this book extraordinary is the honest, humbling transparency that Chris offers, sharing his struggles and failures as well as his victories. It is his honest report of the challenge of actually living this material that gives it so much traction. I have no doubt that the transformation to experience more joy will come to the life of any reader of *The Joy Switch*.

DR. BILL ATWOOD
Anglican bishop and author, *The General, The Boy, and Recapturing Joy*

The Joy Switch is one of those books that can change your life. If you take the time to do the exercises Chris has assembled, there is no way your joy won't grow! Understanding the material gathered in this book will give you a relationship-improving paradigm that you will wish you had known years before.

DR. MARCUS WARNER
Coauthor, *The 4 Habits of Joy-Filled Marriages*

This book is about how to get joy, keep joy, and what to do to get it back when you've lost it. Thanks, Chris, for another great book simplifying complex topics and giving us practical activities to learn the skill of building and maintaining relational joy. Let the relational revival begin!

MONICA MOUER, MS, LCMHCS, CSAT, CERTIFIED EMDR THERAPIST
Center for Family Transformation, Founder and Clinical Director

I am delighted that Chris Coursey, founder of THRIVE and author of *Transforming Fellowship: 19 Skills That Build Joyful Community*, has published his latest valuable work, *The Joy Switch*. With humor and helpful clarity, Coursey demonstrates, encourages, and challenges us to do exercises that cultivate life-giving habits of joy and appreciation, which are foundational skills that galvanize the transformation promised us in discipleship in Christ. *The Joy Switch* is a valuable starting place in the growing Life Model-THRIVE library for those who seek real change and want effective, measurable results.

CYNTHIA JACOBSEN
Soul coach, writer, founder and director of Whole Heart Living

Chris M. Coursey

THE
JOY
SWITCH

HOW YOUR BRAIN'S SECRET CIRCUIT
AFFECTS YOUR RELATIONSHIPS—
AND HOW YOU CAN ACTIVATE IT

NORTHFIELD PUBLISHING
CHICAGO

Scriptures taken from the Holy Bible, New International Version®, NIV®. Copyright © 1973, 1978, 1984, 2011 by Biblica, Inc.™ Used by permission of Zondervan. All rights reserved worldwide. www.zondervan.com The "NIV" and "New International Version" are trademarks registered in the United States Patent and Trademark Office by Biblica, Inc.®

Edited by Elizabeth Cody Newenhuyse
Interior and cover design: Erik M. Peterson
Cover photo of switch copyright © 2012 by kyoshino / iStock (185219319). All rights reserved.
Author photo: Charles Spoelstra

Library of Congress Control Number: 2020945065
ISBN: 978-0-8024-2171-5

We hope you enjoy this book from Northfield Publishing. Our goal is to provide high-quality, thought-provoking books and products that connect truth to your real needs and challenges. For more information on other books and products that will help you with all your important relationships, go to northfieldpublishing.com or write to:

Northfield Publishing
820 N. LaSalle Boulevard
Chicago, IL 60610

1 3 5 7 9 10 8 6 4 2

Printed in the United States of America

I dedicate *The Joy Switch* to my lovely wife, Jen,
who held down the fort during the time I was writing
this book. The time set aside to write this manuscript was
when the coronavirus arrived. The world shut down.
My love, you did the heavy lifting! You covered my
workload, you cared for our children, you led the ministry,
you ran the house and, above all, you stayed relational.
Thank you for living this book out and staying
a source of joy to our little family!

CONTENTS

Foreword..9

Introduction..11

1. Firing Up Your Relational Circuit 23

2. Offline: Recognizing a Shutdown 45

3. Get Back on Track!................................69

4. Removing Roadblocks.............................87

5. How to *Stay* Relational 109

6. Sustaining the Switched-On Life 125

7. Starting a Relational Revival 141

Looking Ahead to Real Life 159

Acknowledgments................................. 161

About THRIVEtoday 164

About the Author 165

Notes 166

FOREWORD

The human brain is an incredible, God-created three pounds of true wonder. It affects our bodies, our relationships, our relationship with God . . . just about everything. And the growing field of neuroscience is helping us understand how it affects our daily lives, including the joy we experience.

Scientists have discovered that one circuit of our brain helps regulate our emotions, specifically joy, and profoundly impacts our relationships. You can almost view it as a switch. The challenge, however, is when it switches off, robbing us of the joy God wants us to experience not only with Him but with those we care about.

Walking with God and growing in our relationships require that we understand this switch, how it works, and how to maximize its impact. *The Joy Switch* does just that.

Chris Coursey incorporates brain insight as he weaves

colorful life stories about his journey in learning about and experiencing this relational switch. He helps us understand how to recognize when this circuit is "off" and when it is "on." He provides a helpful model of the brain's relational circuit. He unpacks how the switch works, what you can do to turn it on, and what turns it off. You'll also learn about roadblocks to joy—and how to stay in the joy state.

You won't find The *The Joy Switch* to be a book of theory. It's a book of practice. At the end of each chapter you'll find several doable exercises you can apply in your life to engage this joy circuit.

If you're looking for a practical book that uses brain insight to help you develop joy habits to enhance your relationships and your relationship with God, then *The Joy Switch* is for you. It's fast-paced, keeps your attention, and provides workable solutions to increase authentic joy.

DR. CHARLES STONE
Author of six books, including *Holy Noticing: The Bible, Your Brain, and the Mindful Space between Moments*

INTRODUCTION

Have you ever lost it—at a time when things were humming along for you?

You were feeling good—until someone said or did *just the thing* to set you off. You got derailed, pushed out of your sweet spot. You stopped listening and started reacting. You no longer felt like a competent, functioning adult, responsible and caring. You turned into that awkward adolescent all over again as fears and big feelings took over.

Of course you have! We all lose it, some of us more than others. No matter how good our intentions or how strong our willpower, we are no match for unregulated feelings. We all reach a tipping point. Our ability to manage what we feel sets the limits on our enjoyment of life and relationships. Under the right conditions, all of us can be pushed too far. But the trick is knowing how to get back to that

11

sweet spot, those healthy emotions. When we don't know how to get back, life becomes unbearable.

Maybe it's the spouse who pushes a button—or all twenty buttons. The children who don't listen. Annoying coworkers who won't stop talking. Disappointment. Fatigue. Rejection. The drive-through messes up a food order *for the second time*. We run late for an appointment, only to realize it's the wrong day.

We all have "buttons"—people or issues that send us spiraling. We reach the point where we feel fragile. Before we know it, we say and do things we wish we could take back. We lose our temper. Some of us slip into depression. Others become anxious. All these have one thing in common: *Someone or something has stolen our joy.*

If you can relate to any of these feelings, congratulations! You are human. You are also reading the right book. You no longer have to stay stuck in the prison of painful emotions and hurtful reactions. You don't have to stay lost during difficult relationships. You can train your brain to bring joy back. With practice, you can help your brain hold onto joy longer. You can make joy your new normal. The exercises in this book are designed to give you practice starting joy.

THE SCIENCE BEHIND
TRANSFORMING YOUR LIFE

My friend Dr. Jim Wilder is a neurotheologian. Jim studies spiritual growth while looking at how the brain works. Jim has spent much of his life creating solutions for trauma and addictions, including the prevention of trauma as well as the development of maturity across the lifespan. There is so much more to Jim's work, but much of what I know about the brain comes from partnering with Jim, who is also the primary developer behind the Life Model, an idealized model for life using brain science and spiritual practices.[1]

In the 1990s, Jim came across the work of Dr. Allan Schore from UCLA. Schore's work shone a bright light on attachment theory to better understand how our relational brain regulates emotions, creates our identity, and runs our relationships. Jim and I started working together in 2001. We were developing exercises and designing methods to train people to learn important relational skills brain science says should be learned the first three years of life—assuming the parents or others are themselves equipped with these skills. When families and communities lack these relational skills, the result is pain, immaturity, addictions, violence, depression, and more ravaging communities.

This book is the result of testing brain-based solutions to help people reach their full relational potential so people live in joy. Learning these important skills keeps us relational with others during good times and bad. We recover when things go wrong. We stay loving, kind, compassionate, and resilient during times of suffering and pain. We rest at the right times. We sustain our relationships during strain. We hold onto our joy.

There is much more to say about the skills, but first we need to learn how to cultivate them—and what gets in the way of becoming relational. My wife, Jen, and I run THRIVEtoday, an organization focused on leading training events and creating resources so leaders, families, and communities learn the nineteen skills. Through our research and experience with thousands of hurting people, we know that the secret to accessing those skills lies in your brain.

Read on.

THE SECRET CIRCUIT

Brain science says you are the possessor of a great gift. This is no ordinary gift. The gift makes people glad you are here. When used, this gift brings smiles, laughter, even warm, fuzzy feelings. This gift is not money, fame, power, or good looks.

Inside your brain is a secret circuit, a relational engine, which goes by many names. Some call it the control center, the relational circuit, or the social engagement system.[2] I refer to it as your *secret circuit* because it's there, but people do not know how to use it. This secret circuit is your brain's relational circuit, which oversees your ability to engage the world—even God. How well this relational circuit is working will have a profound effect on your life. Each of us feels its presence or absence *every waking moment*.

There is only one problem. This relational circuit can easily turn off. When we do not know how to correct this, we are in trouble. Once this brain circuit goes off, we want to find a way to switch it back on. Otherwise, we relationally flounder. This brings us to the Joy Switch.

The Joy Switch is the lever we must pull, the button we must press, to restore the best of our personality, character, and identity. *Here is our ability for joy.* The Joy Switch turns on the relational circuit—which changes everything. How well we use the Joy Switch determines if we reach our full relational potential. This ability is within our reach.

Learning to use the Joy Switch restores the relational circuit so we stay a living reflection of the person we want to be. Otherwise, we relationally explode or we implode. We lose it with family, friends, coworkers, other drivers, neighbors, and more. We "let them have it" or we may beat ourselves up in a sad sort of way. Many of us have inadvertently drifted from who we dreamed we would be. Or who our mother, father, teachers, coaches, and friends knew we could be.

Deep down, we know there is more. Maybe we let the dream die. Maybe we believed the wrong things about ourselves. The good news is, the Joy Switch is accessible so you can start some joy. All it takes is a little direction.

BECOMING WHO WE HOPED WE WOULD BE

How well we learn to use the Joy Switch determines if we recover from upset. The Joy Switch is the lever to unlock our relational potential so we *become who we always hoped to be.* The state of our relational circuit determines if we stay flexible during hardship. If our family and friends want to be near us—or avoid us. Once relational, we can update our brain's "character software" inside the relational circuit to be more resilient. Here we become the person our loved ones are glad to have around. The status of the relational circuit determines how well our diet goes, how much we exercise, if we surrender to our cravings, and whether we resist giving in to what we know we should avoid. It even decides if we feel genuine concern for others or if we've lost that loving feeling.

My hope with *The Joy Switch* book is 1. You learn to recognize whether your relational circuit is working, 2. If not, you know how to use the Joy Switch to turn it back on, and 3. You learn relational habits to sustain the relational circuit so it works at its optimal range.

Learning these three steps can be life changing. Keeping your true self present so you stay fully engaged will take practice. For this reason, each chapter includes practice exercises to apply what you are learning. Now, a little more about me and why I wrote *The Joy Switch*.

UNRECOGNIZABLE—IN A GOOD WAY

When I was in high school, fear ran my life. I wanted nothing more than to fly under the radar and fit in with my peers. I was afraid to speak up in front of teachers and classmates. I avoided negative emotions like shame, so I became a people-pleaser. I feared rejection, so I turned to partying and sports to fit in. I tried hard to make people laugh, to never say no and to come across as if I didn't care. In truth, *I cared a lot*. Because I seemed to be up for anything, people thought I was carefree. I discovered alcohol, and soon I was the life of a party.

I went on to college, but my fears and wild ways caught up with me. I dropped speech class several times because I feared public speaking. I also ended up with two DUI's within a year. I lost my driver's license. I thought my life was over. Finished.

After an opportunity to do an internship with a Christian recovery ministry, my life profoundly changed. The shy, fearful, cautious boy became a confident and kind man who deeply loved others and wasn't afraid to show it. I found joy.

I can't help but share what has transformed me. The material in this book about the Joy Switch changed my life so much, in fact, that I was largely unrecognizable at my last high school reunion. While I resembled my younger self in appearance, my friends could not accept I was the same guy they went to school with years earlier. I acted differently. I was now confident and secure. I was caring. I was present. I gave up my wild ways. At one point, I even pulled out my ordination card to prove I was a ministry man. Who I am today is nothing like the shell of a person I was back then.

Once my wife, Jen, heard the stories and watched the reactions of my friends that day at the reunion, she said on the drive home, "I don't think we would have been friends when we were younger!" I laughed at her words but had to agree. Once we learn important skills we are missing, our brain will run in the most magnificent way. But when we are lacking these skills, we are far from who we could be. Learning new skills can feel as though we have become a new person because we think, feel, and act in a new way. Life will never be the same. The reason I found lasting—and highly visible—character transformation is because *I learned to use the Joy Switch*. You can too.

Thanks to the help of other people who knew how to use the Joy Switch, I learned to find and hold onto joy. To recover from negative emotions, including fear. To rest and stay connected with people during intense times. To be thankful in times of strain. To find God's peace in painful places.

I soon met Jim Wilder, and I learned how the brain runs best on joy. I learned about the brain's ability to stay relationally anchored and its ability to go offline when we cannot manage what we are feeling. As I've mentioned, Jim and I started working together on creating and testing exercises to train the brain to run on joy. I soon developed those relational skills I had been missing. I found peace. I even discovered God.

And with practice, all of us can train our brain to learn new skills.

The Joy Switch jump-started my brain's relational circuitry, which was largely missing during much of my high school and college years. At our core, we are relational beings. The areas in our brain that govern character, emotions, and identity are all relational.[3]

The research behind this important brain system known as the relational circuit has been around for nearly twenty-five years, thanks to improvements in technology that allow the human brain to be scanned in living subjects. The research of Dr. Allan Schore, Dr. Daniel Siegel, and others sheds light on how experience can reorganize neural pathways in the brain.[4] Only recently have people begun to realize the impact changing the brain can have on families and communities around the globe.

Until now, the relational parts of the brain have largely been underestimated and overlooked. We used to think transformation happens with more information, better communication, and good choices. We now know there are actual areas in our brain that respond to specific ingredients found only by interacting with other humans—joyful responses when someone is glad to see us, examples that show us how to handle hardship, a person who helps us rest, and more. It is for this reason I have included practical exercises in this book to help foster these interactions and also help you gauge when you might be going offline relationally. You can put into practice what you are learning.

You, my friend, stand at the front of the line, ready to apply brain science breakthroughs that empower you be unrecognizable, *in a good way*. This translates to more smiles, more joy, more peace, more laughter, more creativity, more generosity—the loving person you always hoped to be.

ENGAGE THE JOY SWITCH—AND ENJOY GOD

The Joy Switch and relational circuit play a crucial role in our spiritual life as well. This "relational circuit breaker" explains why some of us feel closer and more connected with God . . . and some of us feel disconnected. With the relational circuit working, we are fully optimized for relational engagement. When it goes dark, God feels far away, uncaring, even cold. We may feel as if our prayers are bumping against the ceiling and falling to the floor. Even our worship can feel like we're going through the motions. Fellowship becomes painful or dull. This relational disconnect makes the most resolute among us give up. Learning to engage the Joy Switch primes us to enjoy God's peaceful presence, where we discover God is close and caring, even personal and relational. When God's people are fully engaged, we can expect to see a relational revival where good stuff spreads.

GOING FORWARD

The relational circuit sets the limits on what we can handle. It determines if we are warm, engaged, kind, and joyful—or disconnected, rude, checked out, and stuck. With practice, we learn if our relational circuit is on—or disengaged and off. We can learn to be a more resilient, present, and joyful version of ourselves. We can be *fully alive*. Our ability to stay relational sets the tone for every conversation, interaction, meeting, and relationship.

I look forward to our adventure. My plan is to show you how to use the Joy Switch to activate your relational circuit so every encounter is where you shine the brightest!

CHAPTER 1

FIRING UP YOUR RELATIONAL CIRCUIT

QUICK TAKE

Inside our brain is a relational circuit. This important circuit oversees our ability to experience joy and stay engaged with the people we love. As long as this circuit remains ON, we *feel* like interacting with people. We *want to connect*. We are relationally present. The full range of our relational abilities is working. Once this relational circuit goes OFF, we shut down. Our ability to be relational is now diminished. Our thoughts, feelings, and behaviors change. At this point, we are in a different brain state where people feel like annoyances, objects, even enemies. With practice, we can learn to recognize the status of our relational circuit. If we notice we are offline, we can fire it back up using steps I call activating the Joy Switch. In this relational state, glad-to-be-together joy is the fuel for our relationships. The longer we live without joy, the harder it will be to keep our relational circuit running. But simple joy practices return us to relational mode and keep us relational for longer periods of time.

———————————

SO HOW DO WE GET this relational circuit humming again? How can we flip that Joy Switch?

Most of us don't realize we have a relational engine in our head, which influences *everything* about us—thoughts, behaviors, feelings. Learning to use the Joy Switch prevents relational failures, because we move back to relational mode when we "fall out." This action brings out the best in ourselves and in the people we love. Learning to use the Joy Switch is your edge.

With practice, we notice the status of our relational circuit, so we know if we need to use the Joy Switch to return to relational mode. When we, or others, see we are slipping out of relational mode, we can take the steps to restore our relational circuit breaker. Over time, we can learn preventative measures to stay engaged. This is the switched-on life. The Joy Switch exercises in this book provide hands-on practice to stay relational and repair once we go offline. A little bit of practice with joy on the good days provides the reserve we can pull from on the hard days.

I remember a time my friend lost access to his relational circuit because big emotions and upset made it hard to stay relational . . .

WHEN FUSES BLOW

Years ago, I was sitting at the breakfast table with several attendees at a training event.[1] Out of the corner of my eye, I noticed a shadowy figure looming over my shoulder. Before I could figure out the identity of this visitor, I heard a booming voice: *"Chris, I have a bone to pick with you!"* His tone told me this was no joke.

Every person sitting at the table paused their conversations. I recognized this individual as one of the attendees participating in the conference I was leading. Let's call him Mason.[2] One glance at Mason's face told me everything I needed to know: The howling winds of adversity were about to change the course of my peaceful morning. I felt my shoulders tighten. A knot twisted in my stomach. I took a deep breath, then braced for impact.

Mason leaned in and let loose. "How could you play that video yesterday? What were you thinking?" Mason yelled at the top of his lungs. He was now hot with anger; his whole face almost blazed with intensity. Mason's relational circuit was offline. What we call "big emotions" were spilling out.

I quickly realized the short video I had played the previous day about a family suffering for their faith must have set Mason off. *Normally people enjoy this video!* I thought to myself. The video depicted how to stay relational and loving under difficult circumstances. I was unsure why this video bothered Mason so much, but I knew it must have struck a nerve.

I broke eye contact to look at my friends sitting at the breakfast table. Each person looked stunned. Their faces reminded me of deer caught in the headlights of an oncoming car. I knew this situation would require creativity. Mason needed his Joy Switch to access his relational self, which by now was missing in action. In this state, Mason's upset hindered him from noticing all of us had reached the threshold of our ability to stay connected. We were beginning to feel run over by Mason's intensity.

I recognized I needed my Joy Switch to stabilize this situation, so I took a deep breath. I prayed for wisdom. Activating my relational circuit was crucial for what happened next.

INSIDE MASON'S BRAIN

The relational circuit is valuable real estate located on the right side of the brain. This relational engine is a four-level command center, an *emotional control center*[3] that runs our life for success. If neuroscientists could have scanned Mason's brain during this confrontation, they would have seen that his relational engine was severely disorganized. The bottom two levels of his control center had stopped communicating with the higher two levels. Because the four levels are similar to workstations in an office where different areas work together, once one area stops talking with the others, problems arise. This "company" will be in disarray. Now we become emotionally disorganized and relationally disconnected. Our brain shifts from its ideal state of joy to a diminished state where fear, anger, or something else takes over. For Mason, the consequences of this breakdown meant he felt angry, alone, and unregulated—out of control. This was a perfect storm.

All of us encounter perfect storms where we lose it. Our relational circuit can only handle so much intensity before something gives and we "snap." What kinds of things make you snap? Is it when you feel ignored or pushed beyond your limits? Is it when someone disrespects you or your spouse doesn't do something you asked them to do? How well we handle difficulty depends on our ability to manage what we are feeling.

The things that make us snap are precisely what turns off our relational circuit. At this point, we lose our ability to stay flexible and put ourselves in another person's shoes to see their perspective. The "off mode" in the brain's relational circuit is like *airplane mode*, the function that powers down your digital device during a flight. We no longer receive a relational signal to hear what people are saying. There is nothing fun about this breakdown. Most of life can be lived in "off mode" without realizing it, just like you might get off a plane with your device still in airplane mode.

THE DANGER OF BIG FEELINGS

Staying in *relational airplane mode* increases the likelihood we will have ruptured relationships, conflicts, arguments, rejection, and isolation because people don't always know what to do with big feelings—emotions that can quickly spin out of control. Anger that is rising to rage. Fear that is becoming paralyzing terror.

We will look at more Joy Switch examples. For now, it's safe to say: big emotions we cannot handle wreak havoc on our ability to stay anchored. We lose all flexibility and creativity, all ability to be resourceful—all of them essential elements to solving problems. When a breakdown occurs, problems become bigger. Our focus turns to what bothers us. We struggle to quiet ourselves. Unfiltered words fly into our mind and out our mouth. We say or do things we regret. People we care about feel like enemies. We want to win.

Our ability to use the Joy Switch determines whether we stay calm, cool, and collected—or emotionally unfettered, out of control. And Mason? We will return to him in chapter 3, after we learn a bit more about the relational circuit and what your life looks like when it's ON and OFF.

YOU'RE ON!

Consider your ideal day for a moment. What makes it good? Is it because nothing bad happens? You spend the day outdoors in nature? You finish an important project?

You spend time with someone you haven't seen in a long time? Everything goes smoothly without a hitch? Odds are high, one element in your ideal day is when you are with someone you enjoy and they enjoy you.

This means people are glad to be together. And when the relational circuit is fully engaged, people are kind, generous, loving, sincere, and considerate. People light up to see each other. Joy comes easy. So do smiles. We feel thankful. We find it easy to enjoy life. We recover when things go wrong.

The way our brain works, we look back in the rearview mirror of life to predict the future. *We look behind us to predict next steps.* This is the brain's way of learning from history to avoid pain. The approach works fine when we see a life of joy and peace in our rearview mirror. We expect more joy and peace around the corner.

However, when pain, frustration, ruptured relationships, and hardship happen, we expect more bad stuff around the bend. Resignation creeps in. We feel uncertain about the future. We may stop trying or caring. Even give up hope. This is when our relational circuit checks out.

THE BEST VERSION OF OURSELVES

While the relational circuit influences everything about us, we can learn to control it. The goal with our relational circuit is to return to relational mode *as quickly as possible*. Falling out of relational mode is a lot like trying to hold our breath underwater. It doesn't take long before our peace leaks out.

Once our relational circuit is up and running, we regain our ability to be self-aware, flexible, compassionate, understanding, and, above all, *relational*. At this point, we are in the ideal state for joy and peace. This state of being our best is known as *acting like ourselves*.[4] We act like ourselves when we say and do the things that align with our identity. *We reflect who we are meant to be*.[5] We are simply a more creative, relational, likeable version of ourselves. Some would even say we have high emotional intelligence.

Expecting joy

Speaking of joy, the relational circuit comes on when we *expect joy*. Joy is the fuel to run the brain's relational engine. Joy is *glad-to-be-togetherness*, where we light up to see others and they light up to see us.[6] We are the sparkle in someone's eyes.[7] The nonverbal dance of eye smiles makes us feel seen and special. This exchange is more of a reflex than a choice or decision of the will.[8]

Joy is the relational transaction, an exchange with shared glances, smiles, body movements, and voice tones to convey, "I am really glad to see you!" The presence of joy is the turbo-booster, while the absence of joy leaves us on fumes. The relational circuit breaks down when joy runs low. We sputter with little ability to reach our goals and recover when something goes wrong. There is nothing fun about feeling stuck. (Just ask Mason.)

Consider meeting with one of your best friends. What do you expect to see on your friend's face and hear in your friend's voice? What will your friend see and hear from you? Joy! Joy is the ideal emotion for interacting with the people we love. Joy is our brain's sweet spot.

Once we have enough face-to-face joy, we are ready for a pause, the breather that allows rest so we can build more joy. A rhythm develops. We alternate high-energy joy with low-energy rest as two brain states. In this case, being "low energy" is a good thing. But if every time you see your best friend they seem angry, your relational circuit will stay off because there is no joy. We can say the relational circuit gives us *relational superpowers*. We learn to use the Joy Switch to activate relational abilities that turn us into superheroes.

YOUR SECRET WEAPON

One of my favorite grade-school teachers was Mrs. Harris, as I'll call her. This caring woman helped each student feel important. She was patient, compassionate, and kind. I also remember a middle school teacher, whom we'll call Mr. Becker, who frequently lost his temper. He swore in class. He threw things. Mr. Becker even stormed out of the classroom on several occasions. I dreaded his class. Even though I sat in these classrooms over thirty years ago, I can still remember their faces, voice tones, and mannerisms. One brought joy while the other brought sadness—and a little bit of fear! One had a working relational circuit, the other not so much. Can you see the difference?

As I said, a fully functioning relational circuit turns us into superheroes. This doesn't mean we gain a cape and leap over tall buildings, but our superpowers are the *relational abilities, the skills, that allow us to be resilient.* Here is our secret weapon to overcome challenges and pain. Relational skills we have developed over the course of our life are ready to use when we activate the "secret circuit."[9]

Beware kryptonite!

Like Superman, however, the relational circuit has a vulnerability. We are susceptible to a kind of kryptonite, where we lose *access* to our "relational superpowers." Our kryptonite can be a person who is a source of upset, a reminder of past pain, a situation that always ruffles us—say, feeling rejected or let down. Pretty much anything that upsets us and causes a strong reaction has the potential to deactivate our relational circuit. When the relational circuit shifts to the OFF position, we go into this airplane mode state, or what Dr. Jim Wilder calls *Enemy Mode.*[10] Enemy mode is a reduced version of our personality where we become *relationally restricted.* Our relational superpowers diminish. People we normally enjoy feel like enemies. We lose our compassion. This happens a lot in families where spouses can't stand each other. Children resent parents and parents despise children. This reduced state of functioning happens in the workplace, in church, in politics. Everywhere. We have no shortage of examples. All too

The fight to be right knows no end in enemy mode.

often our relational circuit dims and we become indifferent. We give up. Maybe we become numb to the things that used to bother us. We lose energy and motivation to care or "give a rip." We begin to coast on relational autopilot.

Our good intentions and willpower take a backseat to emotional capacity; that is, *our ability to manage what we feel and regulate our emotions.* Qualities like focus, self-control, kindness, patience, and understanding feel elusive, just out of reach. A slew of problems arise with enemy mode. The people we care about become problems to solve or enemies to defeat.[11] Arguments, conflicts, fighting, disagreements, and negative emotions become bigger and more important than relationships. The fight to be right knows no end in enemy mode.

Negative emotions and big feelings happen to all of us. The trick is to learn how to return to being relational. If we know how to use our Joy Switch, the disappearing act of our relational self will be only momentary. How long we stay stuck comes down to *practice and training.* The amount of time our relational circuit remains off is often much longer than it needs to be. Living in enemy mode negatively impacts our personality, relationships, interactions, and pretty much every area of life where we need a working brain.[12]

This "stuckness" leads to the loss of abilities we often take for granted, such as the ability to stay loving, kind, thoughtful, caring, considerate, compassionate, and generous. It means the unwelcome appearance of personality distortions like narcissism, which disrupt relationships and destroy communities.[13] Narcissism is a lot like toxic mold flourishing in our basement, contaminating the air we breathe. Narcissism, the inability to shift out of enemy mode and process shame, robs joy and keeps people stuck in enemy mode. Doesn't this sound fun?

THE JOY GAP

With a working relational circuit, relational joy becomes our new normal, the sweet spot for our nervous system.[14] Glad-to-be-together joy shrinks our *Joy Gap*,[15] *the amount of time between shared states of joy.* The Joy Gap is where we prefer as little time as possible to pass before we grow more joy. A wider Joy Gap means more time passes between moments of shared joy. This hurts! Low joy hardens us in ways we don't like. The presence of joy thaws our character to grow in wisdom and grace.

This "joy shortage" translates to the diminished ability to stay relational while we handle hard stuff. It's challenging to stay relational when joy levels drop. Joy substitutes become alluring. Our cravings increase. We gravitate toward pseudo-joys, the artificial, nonrelational replacements we seek for comfort.[16] Addictions come into play in the form of BEEPS, what my friend Ed Khouri calls *Behaviors, Experiences, Events, People*, and *Substances*.[17] We turn to BEEPS when our joy levels run low.

BEEPS are what we turn to when we feel lonely, overwhelmed, and in need of an artificial substitute for joy and rest. BEEPS compensate for our inability to recover from negative emotions. Some of the more common BEEPS are playing video games longer than we should, watching porn, turning to sugar and alcohol to disconnect, and pretty much anything we turn to when we "reach our limit" and need some type of pseudo-comfort.

What do you turn to after a long day at the office or a painful interaction? Some of our BEEPS are more socially acceptable than others. This reminds me of the time my relational circuit went off—and I tried to eat a dozen donuts.

A DOZEN DONUTS

Jen drove me to the hospital for a procedure where I was given medicine to put me in a twilight phase so I wouldn't remember the procedure. Because I had to fast the previous day, I was hungry. *Really hungry*. On the drive to the hospital we passed all my favorite restaurants. After the procedure, I was pretty out of it. The doctor gave clear instructions: *Whatever you do, avoid acidic and fatty food!* In the moment, this advice seemed reasonable . . . until we drove by all my favorite food places.

I first asked Jen to drive by one particular fast-food restaurant where I ordered a large two-cheeseburger meal, large fries, and large soft drink—along with a ten-piece chicken nugget meal. Then, I asked Jen to drive to my favorite donut place, where I ordered a dozen donuts. My loving wife tried to stop this second (or third) bad decision, but my cravings were high and my relational circuit was offline. Jen planned to eat one of my dozen donuts for herself, which is totally reasonable. However, once I found this out, while still in line at the drive-through, I refused to share my dozen donuts with her! I even threatened to get out of the car and place the order myself at the window. I was way offline. These responses were outside of my character.

Less than an hour later, my senses returned to me and I looked at all the empty food wrappers in the car. By this point I was feeling sick. I said to Jen, "Dear, why did you let me eat all this food?" She turned and said, "*Let* you? Oh, let me tell you what you did!" and I heard a detailed account of what happens when nonrelational Chris takes over. It was not pretty. I gave myself a stomachache and put my wife through a stressful ordeal.

The relational circuit, a type of a circuit breaker in your

brain, is what keeps you anchored to make good and wise decisions for your health. Once the circuit shuts down, the results are not pretty in how we care for ourselves and how we treat others. Decisions can bring unwanted consequences. Take my advice: avoid big decisions, "impulse buys," or indulging in junk food when your relational circuit goes off.

JOY TO BOUNCE BACK

Everyone is going to go offline, like I did, every now and then. But joy gives us strength. This strength grows much-needed resiliency so we resist cravings and bounce back after difficulties.[18] I can remember how hard it was to transition from college into full-time ministry after giving up my partying ways. I started a new job in a new state with no friends and no driver's license. I felt lost! Thankfully, my colleagues and the new community of people I met through the recovery center provided opportunities to grow joy. I felt like I belonged. Eventually, I became a pastoral counselor. I gained my master's degree and started pastoring, writing, and speaking. I went from feeling lost to found; I had a new purpose for life. Joy is a game-changer.

By building joy, we increase emotional capacity, our ability to handle hard stuff. We can even say joy "trauma-proofs" people, particularly our children, so people gain necessary skills to recover instead of staying stuck in painful emotions. Joy is a smile away.

While people may not have the language for the Joy Switch or the relational circuit, those who know us can see and feel the difference when our relational brain is operational or offline. Our face, voice, body language, words, and priorities give it away. The canvas of our body displays clear signals of a relational shutdown. Many of us rage, bite, snap, grump, and blast others with our words and emotions. Some of us are just plain mean in this state. Rigidity takes over. Our face and voice radiate anger, fear, or some other negative emotion. We witness these shifts in ourselves and in others. We can feel a pit form in our stomachs when someone walks through the door and we see their relational circuit is offline.

Sometimes enemy mode is cold and calculating, as we will see in chapter 2. Some of us conceal our distress. We smile on the outside while we rage, worry, or "stew" on the inside. Do you know what you show on your face when you are relationally offline?

Fixing the underlying issues that shut down our relational circuit will improve how well we stay connected during hardship and strain. Sometimes we go offline because unresolved pain is stirred up from something in the present, which reminds us of pain from our past. Other times fatigue, physical pain, or low blood sugar cause a relational shutdown. We will explore more reasons shutdowns occur in chapter 4.

REPAIRING THE DISRUPTION: MEET *CARS*

It is worth noting, the goal is *not* to avoid a relational shutdown. Rather, we want to *recognize, then repair the disruption of our brain's relational circuit.* Learning to use the Joy Switch habits for the relational circuit help us return to relational mode faster. We will explore these useful habits in chapter 3, but the habits to activate the Joy Switch are what I call *CARS* solutions. We use *Connection* to connect with people, thoughts, and situations that stabilize us, *Appreciation* to remember gifts that make us smile, *Rest* to pause and catch our breath, and *Shalom My Body* exercises to calm our mind and body. Using the Joy Switch steps help us shift from shutdown mode back into relational mode. Learning to return to relational mode quickly is what leads to a more accurate reflection of the person we want to be.

With practice, we come up with the language to tell others our relational engine is malfunctioning—we are on the verge of a relational blackout. We utilize the Joy Switch by practicing the habits and doing the things that help us calm and get relational again. As we explore in the next chapter, we can use a wide range of options to activate a fading relational circuit. Some of us need a refreshing stroll out in the fresh air. A chance to spend time in nature, quiet and rest, playing with a pet, practicing gratitude and appreciation, listening to music, talking to a friend, a warm cup of tea, and more can improve the quality of our interactions and help us "stay in the moment."

This is good news! We can learn to activate the full range of our physical, emotional, mental, and spiritual capacities needed to stay ourselves in good times and bad.

THE JOURNEY BEFORE US

The single most important relational habit we can develop is *learning to live with the brain's relational circuit engaged.* Few things are more rewarding than seeing changes in yourself where you relationally thrive instead of falling out of relational mode and missing opportunities for joy. Children feel closer to parents. Marriages have more joy. People feel loved.

Going forward, I will guide you to maximize your relational circuit and remove roadblocks to the switched-on life. You can elevate key practices that activate your relational superpowers.

And now we turn to some simple exercises to activate your brain's relational engine.

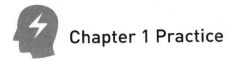 **Chapter 1 Practice**

EXERCISE 1: *YOUR CLEAREST EXAMPLES*

The goal is to find clear examples when you were in relational mode and when you fell out. With practice, you better notice times you are in or out of relational mode. Use a journal or your phone to write out thoughts.

1. Think about a time you were clearly in relational mode; you were your *fully engaged self*. Maybe it was a time you were on vacation, during a weekend outing, etc.

   a. What do you see in your:
      i. Thoughts:
      ii. Feelings:
      iii. Responses:

2. Now, think about a time you fell out of relational mode and it is obvious you were *relationally offline*.

   a. What do you see in your:
      i. Thoughts:
      ii. Feelings:
      iii. Responses:

3. What do the people around you see or hear when you are in relational mode versus times you fall out?

   a. Your words:
   b. Your actions:
   c. Your face and body:

EXERCISE 2: *READY, SET, GET RELATIONAL*

Below are additional questions for reflection. You will go deeper in this exercise if you find a friend or family member to share your thoughts.

1. What kinds of things activate your brain's relational circuit so you are ready for joy?

   a. Example: *Taking walks outside help me feel relational.*

2. What kinds of things set you off and turn off your brain's relational circuit?

   a. Example: *Talking about finances with my spouse, feeling tired, hungry, disappointed, etc.*

3. If you took a guess, how much time do you spend in relational mode in a given day? Check what best applies. Invite your family to take a guess as well.

   a. Note: *Staying in relational mode does not mean you have to interact every waking moment. It means you are relationally anchored in joy and peace, ready to interact if the opportunity arises.*

☐ 0-25% of my day is spent in relational mode
☐ 25-50% of my day is spent in relational mode
☐ 50-75% of my day is spent in relational mode
☐ 75-100% of my day is spent in relational mode

4. What changes, tweaks, or adjustments could possibly improve the above assessment?

   a. Example: *If I went to bed earlier, I would feel more rested and ready to relationally engage people . . .*

5. Glad-to-be-together joy helps us stay relational. Where are the sources of relational joy in your life?

   a. Make a list in your phone or journal.
   b. Now, take 3–5 minutes to remember special moments where you felt relational joy with others. Notice how you feel after thinking about these memories.
      i. You can set a timer on your phone.

EXERCISE 3: *NOTICING THE RELATIONAL CIRCUIT IN MY NETWORK*

We can learn to notice people in our network who excel at living relationally. Here is a good opportunity to interact with people about your observation on *their ability to stay relational.* A direct benefit here is you can identify people who stay relational, you can express appreciation for them, and you gain wisdom from their experience.

1. Identify 3 or more people who appear to be good examples of living relationally.

2. What qualities do you see and admire in each person? Write in your phone or a journal what you enjoy about each person.

3. Make it a point to have a conversation or interaction with each person. Express your appreciation for what you observe. If time allows, invite these people to share how they learned to stay relational. Notice if any patterns emerge.

   a. Were family members or friends involved in demonstrating how to live relationally?
   b. Invite each person to share a time they handled hardship well by staying relational.

CHAPTER 2

OFFLINE: RECOGNIZING A SHUTDOWN

QUICK TAKE

How do you know the state of your relational circuit? The relational engine consists of four levels on the right side of the brain. When we fall out of relational mode, these levels stop working together. Like the car engine that shuts down when fuel runs out, the relational engine in our brain cannot operate. Once the four levels stop working in harmony with each other, we become relationally incapacitated and disconnected.

Learning to recognize our relational circuit means we must first understand the three states the relational brain can have. Once we learn to recognize each state, we can focus on staying relational and correcting times we fall out of relational mode. With practice, we can learn to distinguish the "shades" of our relational circuit to know if we are fully engaged in the ON position, or shut down in one of the two OFF states. Going into "OFF mode" is the brain's version of airplane mode, or what Dr. Jim Wilder refers to as *enemy mode*. The two kinds of OFF mode are *simple enemy mode* where it is obvious I am relationally offline because my words and actions clearly show this. The second is *predatory enemy mode*. In this state, I appear relational, warm, and kind, but I am in a predatory brain state looking to get close to you in order to take advantage of you. You let down your guard because I seem so nice and friendly.

WE HAVE NOW COVERED several important details. One, our brain has a secret "relational circuit," an engine that supervises our ability to stay relational. This is a type of "circuit breaker" that has limits. Once the relational circuit goes off, we utilize the Joy Switch. The Joy Switch activates the key steps or habits to turn the relational circuit back on.

Once online, we gain the brain's full working capacity to navigate life and be our true, relational selves. Once this relational circuit goes off, we lose our ability to fully express our character, faith, and values. Our personality becomes rigid. In this state, we are a poor reflection of the person we want to be. We become a shell of our normal self.

We also know the relational circuit runs on joy. The desire to share glad-to-be-together joy makes the relational circuit turn on and stay on. Here is the best news of all: *each of us is a keeper of the key to activate our relational circuit.* We do not have to stay in the dark. We can flip the switch and on come the lights—as long as we know how.

LANDMINES AND MONSTER MODE

When the relational circuit is running, we feel thankful, plugged in, and flexible. Interactions are satisfying. Once we drift out of relational mode, we focus on problems and pain. Now we are robbed from deep, meaningful interactions. The people we love can feel like enemies. Negative emotions take over. We are trying to survive.

All of us have things that knock us out of relational mode. These "landmines" keep us from relationally engaging the world. Common landmines are the "big six" negative emotions we cannot manage—shame, anger, disgust, sadness, fear, or hopeless despair. Another landmine is the circumstances or people that remind us of pain from our past. Fatigue, disappointment, feeling alone, feeling misunderstood or unprotected, low blood sugar, interacting with someone who doesn't stop to let us rest—all these and more can make it hard to stay relational.

We feel regret and sorrow when we interact with our relational circuit offline because our mouth runs without our brain's filter. It is safe to say we cannot reach our full potential as a parent, spouse, or friend when we shift into enemy mode, what my children jokingly refer to as "monster mode."

In our family, monster mode is a fun reference to describe moments Jen or I fall out of relational mode. However, for many, monster mode is no laughing matter because OFF moments lead to conflict, abuse, bullying, belittling, and many harmful, even devastating behaviors.

Take a moment to think about the faces of those you love. Your relational presence, and the attention that comes with it, is one of the best gifts you can give these individuals.

A LOOK INSIDE THE BRAIN

The brain's relational circuit is a four-level system located on the right side of the brain. This "control center" is largely nonverbal and consists of two upper levels and two lower levels. This is the first system to develop in the infant brain. Until about age four, this system operates as a "separate brain." The relational brain and the verbal brain have to learn to get along after this age.

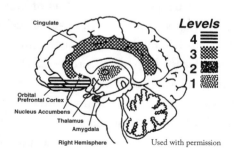

Used with permission

For the most part, we are aware of the activity in the higher levels, compared with the lower levels. The lower levels, 1 and 2, are deeper in the control center, which means we are less aware of what's happening. When the four levels work together, our relational engine fires. We are fully engaged. Any time there is a disruption and we lose our ability to manage what we feel, the lower, nonrelational levels take over. We now lose our ability to stay relational with the people around us. We feel small while circumstances or emotions feel big.

Here is a summary with an overview for each level.[1]

Lower Levels In The Relational Engine

1. **Level 1—Attachment:** The attachment center where we securely (or insecurely) attach to people who share joy and let us rest.
    a. Example: *I bond with the person who is consistently glad to be with me, who lets me rest when I need to.*
    b. Location: *Thalamus and nucleus accumbens.*

2. **Level 2—Assessment:** The guard shack[2] where we watch for opportunities to approach and connect, or fearfully avoid when something threatens our joy. Here is our brain's survival circuit, which is our "self-preservation" center, in charge of the fight, flight, and freeze response.
    a. Example: *If I touch a hot stove, I quickly move my hand without thinking about it.*
    b. Location: *Amygdala.*

Upper Levels In The Relational Engine

1. **Level 3—Attunement**: The emotional regulator where we stay connected in high-energy joy states and coast to low-energy quiet states. Here we use the correct amount of energy to maintain our interactions. We learn to return to joy when distressing emotions arise.

   a. Example: *I walk into the room and notice you are napping so I lower my voice and move quietly.*

   b. Location: *Cingulate cortex.*

2. **Level 4—Action:** The brain's "captain," who oversees our ability to use the best of our brain's resources so we stay creative, purposeful, goal-directed, thoughtful, and resourceful. We act like our true, relational selves using all the best expressions of our identity when Level 4 is running.

   a. Example: *In every situation my Level 4 focuses on staying my relational self whether I am joyful, sad, angry, hurt, or distressed. The Level 4 asks, "How do I best reflect my character and identity in this situation?"*

   b. Location: *Prefrontal cortex.*

THREE STATES OF THE RELATIONAL CIRCUIT

Just like we look up at the night sky to see different phases of the moon, we can look to see the status of our own relational circuit as well as relational indicators in other people. We learn to observe *what qualities are present* as well as identify what is missing as we pay attention to a person's words, actions, mannerisms, and behaviors. Our relational engine is largely nonverbal, so we notice cues such as eye contact, facial expressions, voice tone, posture, gestures, timing, and intensity to see if a person is in relational mode.[3]

For example, Pastor Mike may be a nice guy when he feels happy and things are going well, but once Pastor Mike feels criticized, we see a different version of him—short, snappish, and angry with his team. Staff members around Pastor Mike quickly learn to distinguish times he is in relational mode from times he has fallen into enemy mode and needs space.

The relational circuit has three distinct states: ON, plus two versions of OFF mode. There's the simple version, when we are clearly offline; and the predatory version, where we *appear* relational and warm, but it's all an act, calculated to help us take advantage of other people. In ON mode, the relational circuit is fully engaged and running smoothly. Here is our "sweet spot" where we enjoy the relational abilities needed to run our personality in its optimal state.

Once we learn important relational skills, the relational circuit in ON mode provides *access* to these skills. If we have not yet learned certain relational skills, the absence of the skill will be more obvious once we fall out of relational mode. For example, if I do not recover from my anger, when I am in relational mode my anger is there, but I can keep it in check to some degree. My anger may be expressed with criticism toward myself or toward others, or it could present as frustration when things don't go my way. But once my brain shifts into enemy mode, my anger increases because I just lost my ability to filter my words and regulate my feelings. Self-control flies out the window. Now there is a noticeable change in my language, demeanor, and behavior. You will hear me say words you do not usually hear, and you may see temper tantrums, verbal or physical attacks, and more. A new level of ferocity can appear. Or, you will see me relationally shut down where I lose all ability to stay engaged. I may be frozen, stuck, or locked into anxiety, depression, and more. We can see the "hot" responses such as anger or the "cold" responses where people become callous or even calculating in their words and responses.

HOW CAN I TELL WHEN MY
RELATIONAL CIRCUIT IS ON?

In our book, *The 4 Habits of Joy-Filled Marriages*, Dr. Marcus Warner uses a simple list to determine if the relational circuit is engaged in relational mode.[4] The four identifiers are *Curiosity, Appreciation, Kindness,* and *Eye Contact.* If these four indicators feel true, we are in relational mode and our relational circuit is running. If these four indicators do not feel true, we have slipped *out* of relational mode. This means it is time to return to relational mode.

- **Curiosity**
  - ON: *I can feel curiosity about what people are thinking and feeling.*
  - OFF: *I do not feel curious about what others are thinking and feeling, nor do I want to or care.*
- **Appreciation**
  - ON: *I can feel appreciation in my thoughts and my body. I remember what I feel thankful for (gratitude) and I feel appreciation for the things–people–moments I enjoy.*
  - OFF: *I feel resentment. I do not feel appreciation or gratitude, nor do I want to. I am focused on what bothers, annoys, hurts, tempts, or frustrates me.*
- **Kindness**
  - ON: *I can feel kind and stay tender toward others right now.*
  - OFF: *I would rather win and get what I want in this moment. I don't care how I come across to others. I have no desire to be kind.*
- **Eye Contact**
  - ON: *I look other people in the eye.*
  - OFF: *I have no desire to look people in the eye. I avoid eye contact.*

OUTSIDE LOOKING IN

We all have blind spots. It is often easier for people *outside of us* to notice when our relational circuit is off. Sometimes we are the last to know! Inviting others to speak up when they see we are offline can be beneficial, assuming the two of you have a previously agreed-upon approach that works. I don't recommend the *"Hey, your relational brain is off and it's annoying me!"* method.

In my family, my wife and two sons came up with code words to help one another when we recognize one of us is losing our relational circuit. When my sons were four and six years old, we invited them to help us come up with names we could use for each family member. My sons decided it would be fun to use the name of each person's favorite fruit when we see someone's relational circuit is flickering. Because I like apples, my code word was "Apples," while my wife was "Peaches," and my sons were "Blueberry" and "Strawberry." The guiding principle was this: *any reference to the fruit would be a gentle reminder to use the Joy Switch to get relational, often by taking a pause and a deep belly breath.*

The conversations went like this:

Jen and I to our sons:

"Matthew, strawberry milkshake . . ." and he would shift from hyper or argumentative to taking deep breaths and quieting himself.

"Andrew, blueberry pie" and he would go from whining about something to pausing and quieting to get relational again.

The boys to Jen and me:

"Daddy, apple pie!" and this was my reminder to take a breather if I was getting irritated or going offline.

"Mommy, you need some peaches!" and my wife would use Joy Switch steps to shift back into relational mode once again.

It was humbling having my sons point out moments they observed my relational circuit going offline, yet the results were spectacular. Having the language and steps to recover transformed our interactions. It also helped my sons when they started to argue or whine about something. Of course, there would be times I forgot about our code name system. I would say to one of my sons, "Hey, you are getting hyper. It is time to take some deep breaths and quiet yourself before you get into more trouble!" All too often, my words fell on deaf ears, and in frustration, my relational circuit would start to flicker *because I was focused on the problem*, which was my son's frustrating behavior.

My wife would recognize my error and say, "Strawberry!" and my son would automatically take deep breaths and calm down. It was like Pavlov's dogs! The system worked. We found a language and a style to apply these insights. So can you.

Odds are high, if you do not want to hear from other people about the status of your relational circuit, you are already offline or well on your way. Welcoming feedback (and correction) from others can be a useful thermometer to gauge the temperature of our relational engine. It is worth noting, some people who are already in enemy mode look for opportunities to blast someone by bringing shame or correction. This is unhelpful! Any kind of correction without someone *sharing our experience with us* is not restorative. This brings us to the two versions of enemy mode, the diminished state where our relational circuit is off.

RELATIONAL CIRCUIT OFF: ENEMY MODE

When we shift into OFF mode, this is our brain's version of "airplane mode," where our brain is prevented from receiving signals and updating. Like Mason in chapter 1, we fail to notice we are running people over with our reactions and intensity. We are relationally shut down. We can say our brain's "relational signal" is now temporarily disabled.

As we've already learned, Dr. Jim Wilder calls this brain state *Enemy Mode,* because our brain's relational engine sees others as enemies to avoid or attack.[5] Some of us live our lives stuck in this state.

Simple Enemy Mode

There are two versions of enemy mode. *Simple Enemy Mode* is the most obvious. We are clearly relationally offline, flailing about in a most inglorious way. We sometimes refer to this condition as *Stupid Enemy Mode* because the way we behave is foolish. All of us have said and done some pretty unwise things in this version of enemy mode! We recognize the "stupid switch," which comes on when our relational circuit goes offline. Simple enemy mode is where it is obvious we or someone else is relationally offline, acting in the most irrational, thoughtless, hurtful way. We usually call these people selfish or say they are "acting like a crazy person." It is not pretty—though it is common.

Predatory Enemy Mode

The second version of enemy mode is more sinister because it's cold, calculating, and harder to detect. This version is *Predatory Enemy Mode*. Here people appear to be warm and friendly, in possession of the full range of their relational superpowers. Ah, but don't be fooled. People in this state are cunning in how they think and behave.[6] People pretend to be the relational superhero, all while harboring sinister intentions. This mode can also be called *Smart Enemy Mode* because people do not want their victims to know they are in enemy mode, so they pretend to be "relationally intelligent" by looking like they are fully engaged and caring, while they remain in a predatory state.

In this state, three out of four levels in the relational engine are working in predatory enemy mode—except for the attachment center. This means people appear warm and relational, but they get close to you not because they want to bond and attach but because they want to make you their next meal. Here we see people shift into a most vicious state in order to ambush you and get what they want. Much like the deer hunter who uses a deer call to trick unsuspecting prey, someone in this mode sounds like a loving, caring person in order to draw you in for the kill. You have something they want, and they are motivated to take it.

People can temporarily drop into predatory enemy mode when they try to appease a spouse to get what they want, or placate a boss to get a raise. There are times we can see right through it. But in the more severe cases, we are blindsided and "didn't see it coming." Now we explore these two versions of enemy mode in more detail.

Simple Enemy Mode: Are You Offline?

In simple enemy mode, we lose access to the abilities that keep us relational. We lose all *motivation* to be kind, caring, considerate, compassionate, loving, and patient with ourselves and other people. We are unable to authentically express positive qualities. Our mouth is running and our brain is not updating to notice the effects our words are having. Our thoughts may be negative toward other people. We may smile on the outside, while internally we criticize and tear them down. In this state we are upset, critical, judgmental, and, above all, we want to win! We may blast other people—or we blast ourselves. We see this most clearly with shame reactions. Some of us shame other people in order to punish them. Some of us shame ourselves in order to beat ourselves up.

In this nonrelational state, our brain amplifies negative emotions. Our peace is gone. Problems feel big, even scary. We may want to run and hide from problems or we stay stuck in denial. People feel annoying, threatening, or bothersome. Our cravings skyrocket so we turn to BEEPS (*Behaviors, Experiences, Events, People,* and *Substitutes*) for comfort. We lose self-awareness, so we have no idea how we are coming across—nor do we care!

Below is a short checklist[7] to assess if our relational circuit is offline. When we answer *Yes* to any of these statements, our relational engine is safely *Off*.[8]

- ☐ I just want to make a problem, person or feeling go away.
- ☐ I don't want to listen to what others feel or say.
- ☐ My mind is "locked onto" something upsetting.
- ☐ I don't want to be connected to _____. (Someone I usually like.)
- ☐ I just want to get away or fight or freeze.
- ☐ I more aggressively interrogate, judge, and fix other people.

The above list tells us if we are in simple enemy mode, and the "light" of our relational circuit is off. This list is useful to notice if we are *in enemy mode*. We can also use the four identifiers mentioned earlier to determine if we are *in relational mode*, which are *Curiosity, Appreciation, Kindness*, and *Eye Contact*. (Yes, the acronym is CAKE.) Both approaches are two paths up the same mountain. See which one works best for you.

In simple enemy mode, *people are clearly relationally of-fline and disengaged.* We want to get away from people or problems.[9] All the qualities demonstrating an active relational circuit disappear. Like Mason, we are offline. The people around us can clearly see (and feel) the difference. This shift can happen instantaneously, from a look or tone to something a person says or does which creates a reaction.

High Alert: What Flew into My Car?

One summer day, I was driving when I heard something hard strike the car near the driver's side window. The impact reminded me of times before when bugs inadvertently flew into my car while my windows were rolled down. I grew suspicious. Trying to keep my eyes on the road, I glanced about searching for evidence of an unwanted visitor like a bug or a bee. I immediately looked behind my seat. Nothing. I looked down at my feet. There it was.

A very large hornet was moving around on the floor near my feet. This was the largest hornet I had ever seen! There was no ignoring this creature with a stinger. My body tensed up. My heart raced. I wanted this problem to go away. The survival circuit at Level 2 demanded my attention.

My relational circuit was now offline. I lost all concentration. My breathing was shallow. I felt guarded. All I could think about was getting away from this hornet before it stung me. As soon as I could, I pulled over. In one swift motion, I threw the gearshift into Park, flung open my car door, and leaped out. After a few moments to calm down and catch my breath, I managed to drive the hornet away. My body's fight or flight responses were on high alert. I was out of relational mode and focused on *solving the problem.*

If I were to go down the relational circuit checklist, I would check the following boxes:

☐ I just want to make a problem, person, or feeling go away.
  • *Yes, remove this hornet!*

☐ I don't want to listen to what others feel or say.
  • *Yes, I don't want to talk with anyone right now. Get rid of this hornet!*

☐ My mind is "locked onto" something upsetting.
  • *Yes, the hornet!*

☐ I don't want to be connected to _____. (Someone I usually like.)
  • *Yes, I don't want to be connected to anyone, even my family right now. Get rid of this hornet!*

☐ I just want to get away or fight or freeze.
  • *Yes, I prefer to flee from this hornet. If this doesn't work, I will fight.*

☐ I more aggressively interrogate, judge, and fix other people.
  • *Yes, if I were to interact with anyone under these conditions, my mind would be distracted with the hornet. I have no extra resources or bandwidth to interact with people.*

In this case, of course, there was no harm done, to humans or hornets. But my total fight, flight, or freeze response exactly mirrored what happens to us in simple enemy mode.

Beware the Predator!

As I mentioned, predatory enemy mode is more malicious. In this impaired state, all the levels of the relational circuit work together except the attachment circuit. This means people in this impaired state will not bond well or deeply with others.[10] People interact, not because they care, but because *they are trying to get something.* The relationship becomes a means to an end. People running in predatory enemy mode will often isolate their victims to avoid detection by the victim and his/her group.[11] Isolation makes unsuspecting victims more vulnerable.

In predatory enemy mode, people flatter and come across as friendly and caring so others will lower their guard. They swoop in. The person manipulates. This flawed but dangerous mode is the brain's version of the Venus flytrap. The Venus flytrap releases fragrant nectar so unsuspecting flies will smell the scent, then land on the petals. The insects become ensnared by the rapidly closing leaves, leading to their demise. The flower looks and smells appealing, but it's a death trap. Once people shift into predatory enemy mode, they may pour on accolades, false praise, and deep professions of love as lip service.

All I Want for Christmas

I can remember the time I shifted into predatory enemy mode because I wanted a new bicycle for Christmas. This was no ordinary bike! It was black with white tires and white plastic discs covering the wheels. I pleaded and begged for this bike. I worked extra hard around the house. I finished my outside chores early to impress Dad. I washed the dishes, cleaned my room, vacuumed, dusted, and more, so Mom would notice. My brain was operating in predatory enemy mode to gain Mom and Dad's favor, with one singular objective: *to get what I want.*

I was not sincere in my motivation to be helpful around the house. I was on a mission.

Much to my surprise, I ended up with the bike. But just think about what people are capable of when we desperately want something. How many teenage boys use predatory enemy mode to gain the affections of a girl? How many children rely on predatory enemy mode to bully and cause divisions in order to fit in with friends? How many adults use predatory enemy mode to achieve a goal, land a deal, or attain a status?

Chapter 2 Practice

EXERCISE 4: *NOTICING THE RELATIONAL CIRCUIT IN OTHER PEOPLE*

You now understand the three states of the relational circuit. Identify examples where you observed someone staying relational, as well as examples where you observed someone drop into simple enemy mode and predatory enemy mode. Keep in mind, all of us can drop into the two forms of enemy mode, so the goal is to make a guess based on what you observed.

1. Give examples of times you clearly observed or interacted with someone in one of the three states:

   Relational (On) Example:
   Simple Enemy Mode Example:
   Predatory Enemy Mode Example:

2. Interacting with people in enemy mode can cause us to fall into enemy mode as well. Can you think of examples where you dipped into enemy mode when you encountered someone who was reactive or shut down in enemy mode? What about the situation sent you into enemy mode?

3. Close by thinking about someone you know who spends much of their time in relational mode. What can you learn from this person?

EXERCISE 5: *GRATITUDE GETS US GOING*

Here is an exercise using a Joy Switch habit (appreciation and gratitude) to activate your relational circuit.

1. Think of three things in your life you feel thankful for right now. These may be people, pets, experiences, or shared moments with loved ones.

2. Write on a piece of paper or type into your phone a short name for each gift.

   a. For example, if I am reminiscing about a recent date night with Jen, I may write *Date Night* as the gift I am remembering.

3. Notice how you feel as you reflect on these gifts. Try to think about each gift for sixty seconds as you consider what makes the gift special and meaningful. If you can do this for at least three minutes, you should feel peaceful and more relational. Take the tests below to see if your relational engine is online.

Am I in Relational Mode?

- **Curiosity**
    - ON: *I can feel curiosity about what people are thinking and feeling.*
    - OFF: *I do not feel curious about what others are thinking and feeling, nor do I want to or care.*

- **Appreciation**
    - ON: *I can feel appreciation in my thoughts and my body. I remember what I feel thankful for (gratitude), and I feel appreciation for the things–people–moments I enjoy.*
    - OFF: *I feel resentment. I do not feel appreciation or gratitude, nor do I want to. I am focused on what bothers, annoys, hurts, tempts, or frustrates me.*

- **Kindness**
    - ON: *I can feel kind and stay tender toward others right now.*
    - OFF: *I would rather win and get what I want in this moment. I don't care how I come across to others. I have no desire to be kind.*

- **Eye Contact**
    - ON: *I look other people in the eye.*
    - OFF: *I have no desire to look people in the eye. I avoid eye contact.*

Am I in Simple Enemy Mode?

☐ I just want to make a problem, person, or feeling
  go away.
☐ I don't want to listen to what others feel or say.
☐ My mind is "locked onto" something upsetting.
☐ I don't want to be connected to _____.
  (Someone I usually like.)
☐ I just want to get away, or fight, or freeze.
☐ I more aggressively interrogate, judge, and fix
  other people.

4. Note: If you want to brighten your relational circuit even
more, *share your thoughts* with someone. Expressing what
we enjoy increases our ability to hold onto joy for a longer
period of time. Here is an easy way to spread the "good
stuff."

EXERCISE 6: *CHECKING MY FUEL GAUGE*

Take time each day to assess your current state using either relational circuit checklist. The goal is to recognize if
you are in relational mode and if so, what is going on at
the moment to keep you relational or nonrelational. Write
observations in your phone or journal to see what patterns
emerge.

1. Are there people or situations that cause you to become
more or less relational when you pause to check the
status of your relational circuit?

2. Which checklist do you find more helpful to determine the status of your relational circuits? (See both versions in Exercise 5.) There is no right or wrong answer; this is for your personal evaluation.

3. How does your body feel when you are relational versus times you are nonrelational?

    a. When relational, I notice . . .
    b. When nonrelational, I notice . . .

CHAPTER 3

GET BACK ON TRACK!

QUICK TAKE

We want to learn how to quickly return to relational mode any time we notice we are relationally offline—or well on our way. With practice, we can identify moments we are relationally offline then make corrections, much like we would when we notice we are hungry and we go on the search for something to eat. The longer we stay in enemy mode, the greater our chances of relational casualties. The *CARS* restoration habits are relational "on ramps" to help us reach our destination of relational mode when we are offline. *Connection* is the first Joy Switch habit we will look at. *Connection* is our relational lifeline during times of distress and upset.

SO HOW DID YOU come out on the "test" in chapter 2? By now, you have the language for your relational circuit with some practice under your belt noticing times you are relational or out of relational mode. It is helpful to find your "telltale" signs of what it feels like when you notice you have slipped into enemy mode. In this way, you can quickly recognize moments you are offline and make corrections to return to relational mode.

Life is more colorful and meaningful when we live in relational mode. We better enjoy people. Members of our family, neighbors, the barista, and those who serve us at medical appointments feel like gifts instead of threats or annoyances. My friend Jim Wilder once told me how he fostered a sense of belonging in a difficult setting. His father, Earl, was in the hospital. Jim was worried for his father's well-being, but he sought to remain relational during his hospital visits.

Each nurse and doctor who entered Earl's hospital room received a smile from Jim and words of appreciation when they left. Jim shared with me how, when the nursing staff enjoys being around you, they will enjoy their time in your room. This creates a warm atmosphere where people do not need to feel guarded or tense. We can imagine how, if nurses and doctors walk into the room and receive anger or threats, they quickly lose their joy along with any motivation to stay longer than necessary. When people feel worried or guarded, they are more likely to slip out of relational mode. Because Jim's relational circuit was running, he stayed creative and resourceful during difficulty and brought out the best in other people—which, perhaps, resulted in better care for his father.

I have applied Jim's wisdom with every hospital visit, doctor appointment, and any opportunity to interact with those who serve my family. One day, I put Jim's example into practice when I expressed appreciation to a young man, a clerk, helping me at the grocery store. I noticed his relational circuit appeared to be offline because he avoided eye contact, mumbled something when I walked up, and generally looked like he was having a rotten day. There was no joy or engagement. While careful to avoid overwhelming him, I decided to express my appreciation for his help. By the end of our brief interaction, he looked up and asked, "Do I know you?"

I responded, "No, but I am thankful for your help today!" By the time I left, he was relational, engaged, and smiling. I noticed the person behind me walk up and receive a warm greeting from the clerk. Joy is contagious. Our brain is hard-wired for genuine joy, so a little joy can go a long way.[1] People intuitively notice the effects of relational joy. They may say someone is "spreading positivity" or someone has "a good vibe" or "good energy," when, in reality, living with your relational circuit activated brings out the best in you and in those around you.

WHAT HAPPENS WHEN YOU LOSE YOUR JOY

But it doesn't take long to lose our joy. Within seconds, our relational circuit can shut down. We transition from flexible, patient, and kind to a far less relational version of ourselves. We attack others—or ourselves. We become impatient and demanding. We feel stuck in our pain. The maturity we normally exhibit goes missing, so we become children in adult bodies who throw tantrums when we do not get our way. Have you ever tried to resolve differences with someone who uses anger, fear, or shame to get what they want? What about someone more interested in being right than keeping the relationship? We do not easily forget these interactions.

Some of us turn on ourselves when we lose our joy. We beat ourselves up. We blame, shame, or call ourselves a failure. We may say to ourselves we are dumb, along with more unhelpful phrases we probably heard growing up. We become anxious or depressed. We withdraw. All of us can learn a lot by noticing our thoughts when we shift into airplane (enemy) mode. Old recordings play in our mind. Self-talk takes a negative turn. What is the recording your brain plays when you are relationally offline? Do you place blame on others or yourself?

Staying in our relational sweet spot keeps a rhythm of joy and peace going, while staying in enemy mode is costly. It is expensive to run the brain's relational engine into the red. Everything from our health to our relationships is impacted. Stress hormones take a dangerous toll on our body over time. Thankfully, we can learn to notice when we fall out of relational mode and make course corrections.

THE WAY BACK

Many couples feel trapped in a tug-of-war once the relational circuit shuts down, and winning becomes the primary motivator in a marriage or a relationship. As my friend Alice once told me, "When someone in a marriage wins, both people lose." This is true. The goal is not to avoid the plunge into enemy mode—but to find our way back to relational mode so we regain joy and peace. This transition requires practice because it is a new habit.

As long as we focus on pain and problems, our relational circuit stays off. Learning to recognize and recover from enemy mode becomes a life preserver so we stay present and remain ourselves with every relationship. Imagine what would change in the world if everyone knew how to recognize when they fell into enemy mode and how to return to relational mode? What would change in your family? What about your job or community?

ON, OFF, AND IN BETWEEN

The brain's relational circuit is like a light switch to turn on the lights, but it is more accurate to call it a dimmer switch because it slides to the ON position to brighten a room, or OFF to darken the room. There is this in-between space, a gap, where we may be relational but we can tell we are losing our "relational footing."

Or, possibly, we are in airplane (enemy) mode but slowly warming up and shifting to relational mode. There is a progression with different "relational shades" like colors on a color wheel. For simplicity's sake, I refer to ON and OFF states to describe the relational circuit, but it is accurate to say the relational circuit is like a dimmer switch with shades of relational mode.

I was once leading a marriage retreat when a couple approached me asking if it was possible for a person to live life with the relational circuit off. I said it was; then we talked about the importance of Joy Switch habits to help us return to relational mode once again. This couple was struggling and needed some serious hope. They also needed practical tools to recover. Here is the reason I wrote this book: *living life in airplane (enemy) mode is miserable.* We do not have to be content living our lives relationally disengaged. Hope comes when we believe our dreams are possible. Staying relational gives us creativity, energy, and the drive to achieve the impossible.

Speaking of being relationally disengaged . . . I once fell out of relational mode with my wife when we had a baby on the way.

BIRTHING CLASSES OR BEARS GAMES?

When Jen was pregnant with our firstborn son, she wanted a natural birth, free from medication, so we found a doula.

We also signed up for birthing classes about an hour from our house. I had no real idea what a natural birth meant, but I knew I needed to learn if I was going to be present and useful.

The birthing classes lasted for twelve weeks on Sunday afternoons. Our plan was to attend church in the morning, have an hour at home, then drive an hour for the two- to three-hour-long classes. Sundays were full.

There was one minor glitch in our plans. The classes were offered at the same time my favorite football team played on Sunday afternoons. I grew up in central Illinois, where watching football was a favorite pastime, nearly a religion! Can you see where this story is heading?

I feel embarrassed to admit this, but I can clearly remember conversations with Jen over attending birthing classes or watching football. How well the interactions went depended on my relational circuit.

Relational Circuit On

Chris: "Dear, I am excited for us to do these birthing classes together. This should be fun. I feel sad the timing coincides when the Bears play their football games, but I look forward to doing this with you."

Jen: "Yes, I look forward to doing this together too. I will always cherish this." Usually followed by hugs and kisses.

Relational Circuit Off

Chris: "Dear, the Bears play the Packers today, and my friends are getting together to watch the game. Honestly, I don't feel like going to these dumb classes. I'm really not learning much anyway. I think I can read the workbook they gave us and be fine. Besides, we have our doula with us during the labor, right? She knows what she is doing. The doctor and nurses will be there. Do I *really* need to attend these classes? I think we should stay home today."

Jen: With a sad, possibly disgusted expression on her face, quickly changing to anger: "You signed up for this class with me. You made a commitment. We are going to do this together. How could you say this to me? You hurt my feelings . . ." No hugging or kissing this time. My dimmed relational circuit hurt Jen's feelings, which dimmed Jen's relational circuit. Now we were both offline.

Feeling alone creates attachment pain, the pain of loss.

In this case, what turned off my relational circuit was *not getting what I wanted*. Disappointment and the fear of missing out are easy ways to lose our relational circuit.

My dimmed relational circuit pulled on the bandwidth of Jen's relational circuit, which made it easier for her to lose it. Jen felt dismissed and alone. This may have even activated "landmines of pain" from her past when she felt similar feelings. I was thinking about myself, not my wife or our family. Feeling alone creates attachment pain, the pain of loss. Our conversation with the relational circuit off went nowhere fast.

Thankfully, Jen and I worked it out. We returned to relational mode, and I apologized for my insensitivity. While I missed many good football games, I gained more joy with my wife. This was the relational thing to do! Once my relational circuit was working, I could remember what was important.

Problems become bigger the longer we stay in enemy mode. Now we look at the *CARS* Joy Switch habits to help us return to relational mode.

THE "C" IN *CARS*: CONNECTION

The Joy Switch provides access to our best, most relationally engaged self. Four Joy Switch habits return us to relational mode. These are figurative buttons we press, levers we pull, switches we flip—keys to unlock the door to the storehouse of our relational abilities.

We can use the Joy Switch with the acronym I call *CARS* solutions to reach the intended destination of a working relational circuit. Here is how we drive to the promised land of full engagement. The four *CARS* Joy Switch habits are:

Connection: *I connect with the things and people that stabilize me.*

Appreciation: *I appreciate the gifts that make me smile and feel loved.*

Rest: *I catch my breath and quiet to feel calmed and refreshed.*

Shalom My Body: *I practice exercises to infuse peace throughout my mind and body.*

We will start with *Connection* and explore each habit in remaining chapters. *CARS* is not in chronological order, nor are these the only habits to engage your relational circuit. But they are the most effective for most people. With practice, all of us can discover which habit works best.

Connection is the "C" in *CARS* where we seek the comfort of a familiar face to join us in our distress. We want to feel seen, heard, and understood. Connection is about having someone sit with us. We rely on a person's face, voice, presence, and attention to bring stability and security so we no longer feel alone. Someone is glad to be with us.

Once the connection is made, we no longer feel alone. I can pretty much guarantee my wife is relational and recharged after spending time with her friends. The boost of bonding hormones like oxytocin combined with relational joy is profound for Jen's relational brain!

With connection comes attunement, where we feel seen, heard, understood, and valued. The brain's attachment center, the foundation at Level 1 in the relational circuit, looks for someone we know who will join us in our suffering. This deep connection helps us feel loved so we can return to relational mode. Connection can also be the moments we prayerfully connect with God's peaceful presence to feel seen and understood. We will explore this more in chapter 7.

WHAT MASON NEEDED

Connection brings us back to Mason, who was deeply troubled by the video I had played about a family enduring hardship because of their faith.

While I listened to Mason, I realized he needed connection to no longer feel alone in his distress. I used my words, face, voice, and body language to say, "I'm here with you, friend. I see you!" Connection often leads to rest, so I invited Mason to rest by holding up my two hands to signal a "T" for *Timeout*. I said, "Mason, this is important! I want to hear what you have to say, but can we first pause to catch our breath?"

Mason looked confused. He turned as if he was about to walk away. I said, "Please don't leave! I want to hear what you have to say, but first let's catch *our* breath." Mason cautiously agreed. Notice I said *our breath* in order for Mason to hear he was not alone. Mason stood there while I sat in my chair taking deep breaths. We both needed this pause. The attendees remained at the table, frozen. Sitting there without talking felt like an eternity! Yet the silence provided a needed breather. (This purposeful pause to *rest* is the third element in the *CARS* sequence. We will explore more in chapter 5.)

After a short breather, Mason started to calm down. Connecting opened the door to resting. When I noticed Mason appeared peaceful, it was time for more attunement, which is what we do when we connect with people who are hurting. I validated and affirmed Mason was upset.[2] I could see on his face and hear in his voice how hurt he felt. I expressed my sadness he was offended. I said, "Mason, I am so sorry this happened to you. You are upset! I am sad this happened. If I had known you were going to be this hurt by the video, I would have warned you before playing it. Or I would not have played the video in the first place!"

Mason needed connection and attunement where he felt seen, heard, and understood.[3] If I had slipped out of relational mode and become defensive, or tried to justify myself, this would have been disastrous, much like pouring gasoline on a fire. Mason would have felt alone and minimized. Instead, thankfully, I conveyed, *Mason, I'm with you here. You are not alone. I get it; you are really upset!* Even though Mason perceived me as the source of his distress, I was in a position to share his upset so he felt seen and understood.

Once we fall into enemy mode during conflicts, we often go on the attack. We defend. We justify ourselves. We use our words to inflict pain. Or we retreat and play dead.

CONNECTION SAYS, "I SEE YOU"

As mentioned before, one of the greatest threats to a working relational circuit is feeling alone. We will inevitably feel alone when people try to fix our pain instead of listening, validating, and sharing our distress. Trying to fix upset so it will go away is a classic error well-intentioned people make when trying to be helpful. *People do not need us to fix their distress.* Rather, people need to feel connected so they become relational.

Another classic mistake happens when people try to "talk out their problems" when their relational circuits are off. It is easy to think we can resolve our differences *if only you can understand me/see my position/hear me out.* Trying to talk out problems when we are relationally offline means we will amplify the distress rather than resolve the conflict. All of us can relate to times we tried to resolve a conflict by "getting someone to understand us," only to have the conflict become more inflamed.

After sitting with Mason in quiet and rest, I attuned by validating his feelings. I acknowledged Mason was hurt and upset. Mason needed someone who could stay connected with him during intense emotions. I apologized for the way he felt hurt from the previous day. I watched as Mason listened. With each passing moment, Mason looked calmer and more relational.

In less than two minutes, Mason felt seen, heard, and understood. Mason returned to relational mode. With a smile and a nod, Mason said, "Thank you, Chris," and walked away. Mason's relational engine was firing on all cylinders. I turned to my friends at the breakfast table and reviewed the interaction. "This was a great learning opportunity for you!" I said. While the interaction was intense, the group observed a "live" transition from enemy mode back into relational mode.

At the end of the conference Mason's wife approached me to share appreciation for my interaction with him. She said, "Normally when this happens, we have to leave the conference. But you helped Mason. This week was life-changing for us." Apparently, this video activated a land mine from Mason's childhood where he felt unprotected by his family. When we stay relational, we can join people in their distress without needing to fix it or become defensive. We find creative ways to put out relational fires.

TARA'S TURMOIL

My friend Tara is one of several leaders in a large organization. Tara is good at what she does, but her reactions toward coworkers were starting to erode trust. Falling into enemy mode created problems for Tara.

Tara becomes enraged at colleagues when they fail to meet her expectations. This behavior leaves Tara feeling ashamed and apologetic. When I heard Tara's story, I knew Tara was slipping into enemy mode. Her actions did not line up with her values.

After several discussions, I helped Tara identify reasons behind her reactions. We practiced steps to activate her relational circuit. Tara implemented changes that surprised herself and her colleagues. Here is what I asked Tara to do.

1. Take three-minute breaks throughout the day to catch her breath and assess her relational circuit. (*Rest*)

2. Any time Tara notices she is on the brink of enemy mode, make a point of *connecting* with someone or remember comforting appreciation moments. Tara was a woman of faith, so she frequently used the moment to talk with Jesus *about her upset*. After a few moments, Tara felt more peaceful. (*Connection and Appreciation*)

3. With practice, Tara used the Joy Switch to correct her relational circuit to stay composed and more relational.

Tara's joy levels increased. Her workplace became more peaceful.

We all know people who handle crises like a pro. They stay resourceful, kind, loving, compassionate, and creative. We also know people who fall apart and become selfish, self-centered, rigid, and nonrelational at the first signs of trouble. With practice, all of us can stay our relational selves.

Chapter 3 Practice

EXERCISE 7: *CONNECTION AND APPRECIATION*

We practice the first Joy Switch habit in the *CARS* sequence, *Connection*. We will add *Appreciation* because appreciation keeps our relational circuit on for a longer period of time. *Connection* is where we interact with the people we enjoy—which helps us feel seen, heard, and understood.

We will explore *Appreciation* in the next chapter, but *Appreciation* refers to the joy gifts we remember and savor. We spark appreciation when we watch a sunset, look at colorful flowers, remember a special time with family members, hear our favorite song, or enjoy a cup of tea or coffee with a friend.

If you start this exercise already in relational mode, these steps will feel good, but they will not do much because you are already relational. However, if you are barely hanging on or slipping into enemy mode, you can regain your relational circuits.

1. Assess whether you are in relational mode. Review the checklist below, and if you answer *Yes* to any of these, your relational circuit is offline.

   Simple Enemy Mode

   ☐ I just want to make a problem, person, or feeling go away.

   ☐ I don't want to listen to what others feel or say.

☐ My mind is "locked onto" something upsetting.
☐ I don't want to be connected to _____.
   (Someone I usually like.)
☐ I just want to get away, or fight, or freeze.
☐ I more aggressively interrogate, judge, and fix
   other people.

2. Now, practice the Joy Switch restorative steps below.
   When you finish, review the checklist again to see if you
   are in relational mode.

   a. *Connection and Appreciation*: Come up with 2–3 qualities
      you appreciate about someone in your life, then share
      what you came up with. This works best with a face-to-
      face conversation. Be specific with examples.
      i. Example: *Hey, you were on my mind today, and
         I wanted you to know I really appreciate your
         generosity. When you brought me coffee last week
         it really made my day! I appreciate how you think of
         other people.*
      ii. Notice how you feel after this step.

3. Take a short review to see if your relational circuit is on.
   Review the checklist below. If you answer *Yes* to any of
   these, your relational circuit is still offline.

   Simple Enemy Mode
      ☐ I just want to make a problem, person, or feeling
         go away.
      ☐ I don't want to listen to what others feel or say.
      ☐ My mind is "locked onto" something upsetting.

☐ I don't want to be connected to _____.
(Someone I usually like.)

☐ I just want to get away, or fight, or freeze.

☐ I more aggressively interrogate, judge, and fix other people.

4. If you want to enjoy greater benefits, try this exercise with several people. Notice what happens.

EXERCISE 8: *MY DAILY BREAD*

1. Where in your day did you notice your relational circuit was on?

   a. In the morning:
   b. In the afternoon:

2. Where in your day did you notice your relational circuit was offline?

   a. In the morning:
   b. In the afternoon:

3. Do you recognize why your relational circuit was offline in the "off" moments?

4. Practice this on a daily basis for a week and see what patterns emerge.

5. Find someone you trust with whom you can share your findings. Use your observations as an opportunity to express the "relational qualities" in them that inspire you.

REMOVING ROADBLOCKS

QUICK TAKE

Much like removing a splinter so a wound can heal, we can learn to identify and disarm relational roadblocks that continue to keep us locked in airplane (enemy) mode. Everything from feeling threatened to unresolved pain, loss, physical needs, and missing relational skills can cripple our ability to stay relational. We reviewed the "C" for *Connection* in the *CARS* sequence, so we now turn our sights to the "A" for *Appreciation*. We close this chapter with a look at how to stay relational with people who are offline.

THE LONGER WE STAY stuck in enemy mode, the harder it will be to make our relationships work. In this weakened state, our relational capacities are severely limited. The goal is to *stay in relational mode* and quickly recover when we fall out. We do not have to fear slipping into enemy mode, but we do want to be equipped to return to relational mode quickly.

What would change if you checked your relational circuit before a big meeting, important conversation, when you woke up each morning, before you arrived home to greet your family, when your cravings were surging, before appointments with people, and prior to every interaction with another human being? For the spiritual-minded, what would change in your walk with God if you were in relational mode with the full range of your emotional, mental, physical, and spiritual abilities? Your brain would search for peace and joy instead of focusing on problems. *Thinking about problems and pain turns off your brain's relational circuit.* This creates the worst conditions to interact, focus, learn, and listen.

WHEN THE FUSE IS TOO SHORT[1]

Not long ago, I was driving down the road when I encountered two men in enemy mode. They were ready to kill each other!

The look on his face told me the fellow was about to lose it. He confirmed my suspicions when he jumped off his bike, ripped off his helmet, yelled obscenities, then flipped the driver the bird—with both hands. I felt my body tense up watching this interaction unfold.

Moments before, I had pulled up to the intersection and watched as the bicyclist was about to cross the four-way intersection. An elderly man pulled up in his minivan. The driver had to be in his eighties, and he stopped where the bicyclist was beginning to cross. I watched as the driver became agitated because the bicyclist was now crossing the road where he was about to turn. My guess is, the van driver felt he had been cut off by the cyclist and did not realize bicyclists have the right of way. Instead of yielding, he probably wanted to get moving. I suspect he was already in enemy mode because he was impatient from the start. *He did not want to wait* for the cyclist to cross the road! The driver looked annoyed. He honked his horn. Things went south from there.

The sound of the horn sent the cyclist into simple enemy mode. He flew into a frenzy. In a flash, he became livid and out of control. The cyclist leapt off his bike and ran after the van yelling, gesturing, and looking like a madman on a mission. I was relieved when the van quickly drove away. This cyclist was ready to pounce.

I reflected on the frequency of interactions like this, where someone or something sets another person off and a blowup ensues. I see this happen on roadways, in airports, grocery stores, parks, even ministry meetings and church parking lots. People struggle with short fuses, or they become fearful and stay locked up over the things that frighten them. When we lack skills to stay relational, we remain stuck in enemy mode. Enemy mode is our brain's solution to self-preservation where we prepare to fight, flee, or freeze. We solve problems by attacking another person (fight), or we avoid conflict (flee), or we shut down (freeze). This brings us to Angie, who was afraid of failing.

WHAT IF I FAIL?

My friend Angie was preparing to graduate from school, but she had an upcoming test for one of her classes. This test was crucial for Angie to pass her class and graduate on time, but it was also very difficult. The pressure triggered a strong fear response in Angie.

Angie became increasingly worried. Fear over this test hindered Angie from staying relational. She wanted to run! Instead, Angie turned to sugary foods for comfort. Sleep was spotty at best. Angie lost all desire to go out with friends and do fun things to take her mind off the test. She felt like staying in bed and watching movies. Angie frequently shed tears and broke down over what seemed like minor irritations. All she could think about was failing her class and facing her parents.

Angie would later realize this important test reminded her of the time her parents divorced and she felt like she had to choose sides. This meant disappointing one of her parents. The pressure she felt at the time was excruciating. Though this happened years earlier, some of the unresolved pain, a "landmine," was now activated. Thankfully, Angie reached out to an old counselor for help. This person helped Angie feel understood so she could see how her past was sneaking into her present. (*Connection.*) Angie made a list of the moments, things, and people she enjoyed, which calmed her mind. (*Appreciation.*) Angie would go on to pass her test and graduate with her friends.

We can "extend" the wick of our fuse by building relational joy and increasing our emotional capacity.[2] We sustain the shelf life of our relational circuit when we disarm hidden landmines, the unprocessed pain memories, which cause big reactions and blow up our relationships. But we also need to acknowledge the truth: relational living is *hard*.

DISARMING THE "RELATIONSHIP BUSTERS"

Many things neutralize the relational circuit. What deactivates the relational circuit comes in all shapes and sizes. Everything from recurring arguments, feelings of rejection, minor but nagging annoyances, alcohol, fatigue, physical pain, low blood sugar, to a mere look or a certain tone of voice, can push us into enemy mode. Sudden reminders of unresolved pain from the past can quickly deactivate the relational circuit. When pain from our past sneaks into the present, our reactions are big and emotions run high.

We may not understand *why* we lose our relational footing, but there is a reason. Or, actually, a number of reasons. Gaining insight into this dynamic may initially feel like trying to solve a mystery, yet with some exploration, we discover hidden blocks that sabotage our ability to stay relational. We disarm these "relationship busters" when we know what to do. Here is a look at these roadblocks.

Roadblock #1—Threats to Self

As the above example illustrates, any time we feel threatened, the brain's survival circuit kicks into high gear. We are ready to fight, flee, or freeze. The survival circuit assesses whether we can fight our way out—or whether we need to run. If we cannot outrun the threat, we shut down and freeze, with the hope we will be around once the threat disappears.

Here we see how friction and tension between peers, or in the workplace with coworkers, can lead to active conflicts. When someone feels insecure or threatened by someone, he or she may respond by going on the offensive and attacking. Gossip, slander, ridicule, and bullying are done by people who are in enemy mode. This pain leaves victims caught in enemy mode as well because they are now afraid of being hurt, or they are angry and ready to retaliate.

ROADBLOCK #1 QUESTION:
What threats or fears hinder your relational circuit?

I remember my friend Tim telling me how badly he used to stutter in grade school. Tim's peers were unrelenting in mocking him. Tim feared going to school. When he did go to school, he tried to hide and stay undetected. Feeling anxious and self-conscious made Tim's stuttering worse, so speaking up in class felt like torture; then more bullying made his stuttering worse. Trapped in a vicious cycle, Tim felt alone in his pain. The anxiety around speaking left Tim living most of his life in isolation with his relational circuit offline. He gravitated toward nonrelational activities later in life, such as woodworking in his basement and spending most of his time working in his yard to avoid relationships. Tim's experience taught him people were not to be trusted.

In Tim's case, he turned inward with his hurt and anger. In other instances, victims of bullying all too often turn their anger outward, resulting in acts of retaliation that make the evening news. When we feel threatened and emotions run high, enemy mode is ready to solve the problem.

Roadblock #2—Unprocessed Pain

We're all familiar with trauma and the scars it leaves on those who have suffered its impact. Maybe we've suffered trauma ourselves. According to research by the Life Model,[3] an organization that explores a wide range of psychological and spiritual issues, there are actually two "types" of trauma: Type A and Type B.[4] Type A Traumas are *painful absences* that stunt personal growth. Here we see the lack of joy, not feeling loved, not receiving enough healthy touch, and the failure to meet our physical, mental, and emotional needs take a toll on our brain's ability to be relational.[5] These painful absences create deep pain and cover a wide range of hurts, from the lack of love to little connection, and more, which was needed but unavailable.

Next are the B Traumas, which are *bad things that should never happen*. Here we see abuse of all kinds, natural disasters, and pretty much the stuff we normally think of as traumatic. Both are painful, and both kinds of trauma stunt our growth and make it difficult to stay relational.

ROADBLOCK #2 QUESTION:
Where does unprocessed pain rob you?
Where do you see oversized reactions in yourself and the people around you?

When our needs are neglected (A), or bad things happen (B), our ability to recover and live relationally is damaged. Recovering and processing this pain comes down a number of factors, from our working emotional capacity (joy) to the strength and skill required to process pain.[6] Trauma results when something is too big and we are too small. As we grow older, our bodies grow but we stay emotionally stunted. Unprocessed pain is the result of unfinished processing of painful events in life that become uninvited guests in the present.[7] *What this means is unresolved trauma sneaks in undetected.* We react without fully understanding why. Like Angie, we end up with large reactions to what seem like minor irritants. Overreactions in the present are often connected to past pain that keeps us in enemy mode. These reactions can be the breadcrumb trail to help us identify our pain so we can heal.

Roadblock #3—Loss

When Jen and I were first married, there were times I would cancel our date nights. In my mind, this change was not a big deal. I assumed we would simply reschedule our date for another time. In Jen's mind, however, this was a very big deal.

Any time I canceled our date night, this change created distress for Jen. So much, in fact, we would often argue and fall into nonrelational conflicts over the date night dilemma. From my perspective, Jen was overreacting. It was that simple!

From Jen's perspective, she did not feel valued. Nor did she feel heard by me. She would often say, "If I was important to you, you would not cancel our date nights! You are making something else more important than me!"

In truth, I *was* being dismissive. I assumed if it was not a big deal to me, it would not be a big deal for her. I would often become defensive and shift into enemy mode when I felt she was questioning my motives. I did not understand how my cancellations were making Jen feel unimportant.

Nor did I see how changing our plans reminded Jen of times in her life where she felt insignificant. We bumped into some unprocessed pain here, yet there was one added ingredient that made this situation worse: *loss*. Jen felt alone and unloved in those moments I canceled our date nights. There was no talking our way out of this one. Thankfully, as I worked to return to relational mode, I could put myself in Jen's shoes and see her perspective. And, as Jen recognized some of her past pain, she could better manage her big feelings and stay relational. We worked it out.

One ingredient we can count on to hinder our ability to stay relational is loss. Loss, or *attachment pain*, is what we feel with rejection, abandonment, isolation, death, divorce, and other situations where *we feel alone or we lose something important to us*. Loss could fall under unprocessed pain, but it is significant enough to have its own category.

Loss creates the toughest conditions for the relational circuit to stay on. Feeling alone, thinking about, and remembering loss turns off the relational circuit. It will be hard to jump-start the relational engine as long as attachment pain is present. Loss is behind the more violent and severe reactions we see in the world.[8]

Loss, and the lack of responses to our needs, exact a heavy toll on our ability to stay connected. Loss amplifies pain at each level in our relational engine. This means loss creates more intensity when we are upset, loss makes it difficult to rest, loss makes it harder to stay connected with others, and loss makes it hard to remain our relational selves. The day after a short night of sleep may be difficult, but the day after a short night of sleep *when I'm grieving a loss* is much harder. The pain of loss not only puts us in enemy mode, it propels us to use pseudo-joys for comfort.

ROADBLOCK #3 QUESTION:
Where does loss or the fear of loss run your life?

Staying connected with the people we love provides endurance to suffer well during hardship. *Our relational circuit is more likely to stay on during distress when we have people who are glad to be with us.* Everything from the fear of rejection to the hidden, but present, attachment pain will make it hard to stay relational.

Roadblock #4—Physical Needs

Physical needs refer to self-care and the wide range of needs that impact our brain and body. How well we care for ourselves contributes to our ability to stay relational. One common roadblock I recognize in Jen, for example, is when her blood sugar crashes. If Jen has not eaten in a while, I can tell by the tone of her voice she is shifting into enemy mode. Hearing her voice tone alerts me to investigate when she last ate—or if she needs a snack to increase blood sugar levels. It is nothing short of remarkable how quickly she recovers once she eats a snack! Because of this, we have learned to stay proactive and bring snacks on trips when we travel.

> ### ROADBLOCK #4 QUESTION:
> *What sorts of physical needs or weaknesses send you spiraling into Enemy Mode?*

For me, Jen has learned to detect I am slipping into enemy mode when my back pain starts to intensify. For several years now, I have suffered from a back injury. Jen can tell by the look on my face when an ice pack is needed. A nagging back injury provides useful fodder to practice the Joy Switch habits mentioned in this book.

Learning to pay attention to our bodies and tend to personal needs can prevent and minimize relational blowouts. We want to learn how to be tender with the weaknesses in our midst.[9]

Roadblock #5—Missing Relational Skills

Jen and I lead an organization called THRIVEtoday, which trains people in nineteen relational brain skills through exercises and interactive training.[10] We train leaders and communities to learn foundational skills needed to make our brains and relationships work. *Each of us must learn to use relational skills to recover when things go wrong to stay our best selves during pressure and strain.* These are skills to keep relationships bigger than problems. Without relational skills, our relationships will suffer. Relational skills strengthen the relational circuit to be fully equipped so we stay resilient and maintain our character values in good times and bad. We can expect to see a trail of broken relationships in the wake of our lives when relational skills are absent.

We learn relational skills by interacting with people who already have relational skills. These are people with more training in specific areas. For example, if you can return to joy from your anger, you are now a resource to help me learn the skill. If I can stay my relational self when I feel shame, I can be a resource for you. We need each other. Relationships are opportunities to grow our skills and reach our God-given potential.

> ### ROADBLOCK #5 QUESTION:
> *What relational skills are missing,*
> *hindering my ability to stay relational?*
> (You can see the full list of relational skills at thrivetoday.org.)

Much like learning to play the guitar or pick up the game of golf, we need practice and guidance to show us how to learn new skills. This step-by-step practice with experienced minds demonstrates how to do something in a new or a better way. We may ask, "How do you recover so well from your anger? Tell me a story." Or, "Why are you so joyful?" and, "How is it you can stop when you see someone reach their limits? What do you see when people are maxed?"

Relational Skills in Action

I remember watching my friend Dr. Jim Wilder handle a difficult interaction. Jim was a speaker at a conference, and I was there to run the book table. A person approached Jim and started talking to him. The fellow was rude. I remember sitting there watching this interaction, waiting for Jim to "put this guy in his place." I quickly recognized I would have shifted into enemy mode. I was baffled how Jim stayed his relational self. Jim remained kind and polite; tender with the man's weaknesses.

Jim kept his relational circuit on and used a number of relational skills I did not yet have. Observing Jim provided a helpful example for me. When I was in similar situations later in life, I could ask myself, "How would Jim handle this?"

Once relational skills are missing or undeveloped, we compensate with nonrelational strategies. We lose our ability to recover from upset. Any time something offends or annoys us, we forget who we are, just like the bicyclist who lost his cool with the elderly driver. We are unable to stay tethered to our identity and character in enemy mode. We lose our ability to reflect our best qualities. Negative emotions take over.

THE "A" IN *CARS*: APPRECIATION

As we look at the *CARS* of returning to relational mode, we have so far learned the Joy Switch habit for *Connection,* which keeps us engaged with people we trust so we can "borrow" some of their bandwidth to regain access to our relational circuit. This means when I feel maxed out and relationally offline, I connect with someone who is relational, who can listen, attune, and help me feel seen and understood so I can then return to relational mode.

When we calm down and return to joy from a negative emotion, our brain develops a pathway back to relational joy. In this way, we do not stay stuck in our upset. We learn to reach out and connect with others when we feel alone. We ask for what we need. We learn to rest when we need a breather so we take the purposeful pause as we need it. No matter where we are in our ability to live relationally, each day is an opportunity for practice. Each interaction is an opportunity to grow our skills—if we know how.

And now, we look at our next Joy Switch habit, *Appreciation*.

Appreciation, what I call *packaged joy*, is what happens when we unwrap joy gifts. These are the special moments; memories of the people, interactions, sights, sounds, smells, textures, and tastes that spark a smile.[11] Remembering and feeling appreciation activates our relational circuit. In addition to packaged joy, we can feel gratitude and use thankfulness to stay relational. Appreciation and gratitude provide much-needed sparks to fire up our relational engine. We can unwrap packaged joy presents and feel grateful whenever we want—they are free!

Making a list of the moments, people, and things we appreciate provides a useful tool when our relational circuit starts to dim. During moments we notice our mood is going south and we are becoming anxious, angry, or tense, we recall a meaningful interaction or a special moment. Then, we think about these times. We feel the emotions in our body. For me, when my relational circuit is going off, I pull out an appreciation journal or view pictures on my phone to reflect on special times. I may remember moments with my sons or the time Jen and I enjoyed a date night walking along Lake Michigan, or I recall the time I observed ducks waddling around my yard. I notice how my body feels; and, if I really want to fill up on the appreciation feelings, I share the story with a friend or family member.

Opening "joy files" by thinking about the good stuff starts a chain reaction in our brain and body where we respond as though we are reliving the moment all over again. Our sadness turns to joy! The brain trained on appreciation and gratitude will search the environment for good things to enjoy, while the untrained brain will look for things to criticize and complain about. Appreciation is the practice that increases neuronal density in one of the most complex regions of the brain.[12] This means those who regularly practice gratitude require less effort to be grateful because it is a habit.[13] The practice makes brain neurons more efficient so a new normal develops. Gratitude changes our brain and relationships![14]

We can think of packaged joy as our *relational oxygen mask* to navigate emotional turbulence. Appreciation anchors us during troubled times. Dr. Jim Wilder suggests a compelling exercise where we feel appreciation three times a day for five minutes each time, for a total of thirty days. Doing this exercise resets the thermostat in our nervous system and recalibrates us for joy and peace.

I can make a habit of remembering the good stuff to be refreshed and relational.

We can ask ourselves, *What do I feel thankful for today? What good things can I remember that make me smile? What brought peace?* Make your list. Enjoy the moment.

STAYING RELATIONALLY AFLOAT WHILE OTHERS ARE DROWNING

CARS can help us throw out a life preserver when we see someone struggling relationally. When we see a person drowning, we should not jump in the water to rescue the person *unless we are highly trained*. The drowning person's survival circuit is in charge. This means they can inadvertently pull us under the water. Their brain is in enemy mode, trying to preserve self.

Instead, we should toss a life preserver, call for help, or find a long pole to help the person reach safety. The same is true with airplane turbulence. If we are in an airplane and there is trouble, oxygen masks drop down from the ceiling. We put the mask on before helping people around us. We can learn from these safety guidelines when it comes to staying relationally afloat when people around us are drowning. *Our job is to stay relational* when we encounter someone in enemy mode.

When people around us plunge into the icy waters of enemy mode, it can be difficult to stay relational because *their nonrelational state* triggers our fear, activates our pain, and brings up our own nonrelational reactions. This can cause us to slip into enemy mode. Soon, both of us are sinking. Instead, our goal is to *remain our relational selves.* Do not try to fix the person; rather, practice the *CARS* Joy Switch steps and invite those who are drowning to do the same.

Here is a good opportunity to help people feel connected, seen, and understood. Once someone feels connected with you, it's a good time to invite the person to practice appreciation and gratitude for a relational refresher. When you stay relational, you give someone in enemy mode the best chances of recovering. Staying relational is one of the best gifts we can give others when we see they are drowning in their distress. I appreciate the wisdom from the Bible, that we should " . . . be quick to listen, slow to speak and slow to become angry" (James 1:19b). Here is wise advice for all our relationships. If our relational circuit is working, we will be good listeners, we can rest, and we avoid overreacting.

 **Chapter 4 Practice**

EXERCISE 9: *THE ABC'S OF APPRECIATION: THINK, FEEL, SHARE*

We practice the next habit in the *CARS* sequence, *Appreciation*. Feeling appreciation activates the relational circuit. When we make appreciation a habit, we teach our brain to scan for good things to enjoy and expect good things in the future. The painful absence of appreciation leaves us feeling resentful and critical.[15] We maximize appreciation when we think about the good stuff, feel the good stuff, and share the good stuff.

1. First, assess whether you are in relational mode. Review the checklist below. If you answer *Yes* to any of these, your relational circuit is offline.

   Simple Enemy Mode
   ☐ I just want to make a problem, person, or feeling go away.
   ☐ I don't want to listen to what others feel or say.
   ☐ My mind is "locked onto" something upsetting.
   ☐ I don't want to be connected to _____.
     (Someone I usually like.)
   ☐ I just want to get away, or fight, or freeze.
   ☐ I more aggressively interrogate, judge, and fix other people.

2. Make a list of 10 things, moments, and people you appreciate. Create a list on your phone or in a journal. Give each a short name.

   a. Example: my morning walk listening to the birds sing may be named, "Walk with birds."

3. When you finish your list, scan how you feel in your mind and body. What do you notice? Review the checklist above to see if you are relational. Keep in mind, *Yes* to any of these means your relational circuit is still off.

4. Find someone with whom you can share your appreciation list. Invite this person to share special moments he or she feels thankful for. See what you notice.

EXERCISE 10: *UNWRAP PACKAGED JOY*

We now activate specific joy moments. Thinking about joyful times opens the "joy file" in your brain so your body responds as though you are reliving the moment all over again. The useful sequence to maximize appreciation is to 1 - recall the moment, 2 - feel the feelings, then 3 - share the story.

1. Think about your favorite memories involving:

   a. People: spending time with the people you love.
   b. Places: going somewhere special.
   c. Food: eating something you enjoy.
   d. Animals: your favorite pet or an animal you enjoy.

2. Next, write down a name for each moment and share stories with family members and friends.

3. Notice how you feel after accessing these joy files. Do you feel more relational?

4. Check the indicators chart below to see if you are in relational mode. If you answer *Yes* to any of these, your relational circuit is off.

Simple Enemy Mode

☐ I just want to make a problem, person, or feeling go away.

☐ I don't want to listen to what others feel or say.

☐ My mind is "locked onto" something upsetting.

☐ I don't want to be connected to _____. (Someone I usually like.)

☐ I just want to get away, or fight, or freeze.

☐ I more aggressively interrogate, judge, and fix other people.

5. Make an ongoing list of good things from your day and share your list with others on a regular basis.

CHAPTER 5

HOW TO *STAY* RELATIONAL

QUICK TAKE

Creating new habits take time. The goal is to train our brain to learn how to stay relational. We want to reach the point where we clearly notice moments we slip out of relational mode and take the steps to quickly return to relational mode—the faster, the better. The more we practice this sequence, the better trained our brain will be at staying relational and recovering when needed. We can learn to use the *CARS* habits without thinking about it. We can learn the cues which tell us we or others have fallen out of relational mode. In order to stay anchored over time, we must rest. *Rest* is the third Joy Switch habit. Rest is the purposeful pause to quiet our mind and body. Taking a short breather keeps us stable and helps us return to relational mode. Rest is a foundational skill for strong mental and emotional health. It is also a quickly fading skill. But with practice, we can learn how to insert this important habit back into our families and communities.

_____

WE NOW HAVE THE *CARS* habits to help us *return* to relational mode. But why do we "go offline" in the first place?

Learning to *stay* relational is one of the greatest relationship skills we can ever learn. Every area of life will be enhanced by our ability to remain engaged. This process of restarting the relational circuit may feel daunting at first, but it is not difficult *if we make it a habit.* I refer to habits and skills interchangeably. Both habits and skills help us keep relationships bigger than pain or problems. Both must be practiced in order to be learned.

While the *CARS* habits are also skills we must learn, the main focus of the *CARS* habits is *to return us to relational mode. CARS* are learned habits, what we can consider to be a subcategory of the nineteen relational skills, that larger set of skills that make our relationships work. Learning to turn on the relational circuit is "Skill 0" in the nineteen skills. (Visit thrivetoday.org to view the full list of skills.)

THE FAST TRACK IN YOUR BRAIN

Creating new habits requires time and practice. The goal of a habit is to make an action a "reflex" where we do something without thinking about it. Joy-based habits engage the relational circuit, which is a superhighway in the brain, what Jim Wilder and Marcus Warner call the "fast-track" processor in their book *RARE Leadership*.[1] As Wilder and Warner say, the fast track in the brain uses white matter instead of grey matter. Ingrained habits use white matter in the brain, and white matter runs two hundred times faster than grey matter.[2] Habits learned in the fast-track system are more like reflexes because we do not need to think in order to act.[3]

When we have to think about something in order to make a decision to act, this process engages the "slow-track processor" in the brain, which relies on grey matter.[4] The brain's slow-track processor is a horse and buggy compared to the fast track. The fast-track system in the brain is where we create new habits, the reflexes, which help us respond to the ever-changing needs within our relationships. These habits become ingrained responses to keep us relationally engaged where we adjust as needed to people, faces, and circumstances. In this way, I can pause when I see you are reaching your limit. I quiet when I reach my limit. I use relational skills to stay connected in good times and bad. We often take these "abilities" for granted without ever realizing our brain had to *learn* these important skills by interacting with others who already had the skills.[5]

As we have emphasized, using the Joy Switch to turn on the relational circuit provides access to the nineteen relational skills that make our relationships work. Of course, when we have not learned a specific relational skill, we compensate with nonrelational substitutes. When I do not rest, for example, I may turn to other avenues to disconnect. I may plug in and get lost in social media, entertainment, video games, overworking, keeping busy with distractions, and more unwanted behaviors to try to turn off and disconnect. Even good things can become unhealthy when we use them to substitute for the real thing.

GETTING GOOD AT STAYING RELATIONAL

We now look at two ways to stay relational. First, we notice how relational mode feels so it becomes our new normal. Second, we notice when our joy is fading and our relational circuits are going off. We want to be really good at these two practices!

First: Learn How It Feels

To learn how to stay relational, we must first learn *how it feels* when we are fully engaged in relational mode. What do you see? What do you hear or feel when you are relational? How would you describe it?

For me, colors appear brighter. Sounds clearer. Textures richer. Tastes are better and more enjoyable. I feel peaceful. I can breathe easy and deep from my belly instead of my chest. I enjoy people. Do I feel **curious** what others are thinking? Can I feel **appreciation** right now? (Can I think about the good stuff and feel it—or do I revert to mulling over the things that bother me?) Do I want to be **kind**? Do I maintain **eye contact** with others?

Once we are familiarized with *the feeling* of relational mode, we compare how it feels when we are in airplane (enemy) mode. We may notice enemy mode feels smothering. Is there tension in your body? How is your breathing —shallow or relaxed? Are your reactions rigid and stiff? Do you want to win arguments with others? In the moment, pain and problems may feel more important than the people you love. Cravings feel intense, even overpowering.

The goal is to become familiar with how good it feels to be in relational mode. This makes it easier to notice when we shift into enemy mode because our joy is fading. Recognizing the signs I am falling out of relational mode reminds me of the time I hit a patch of black ice.

Second: Notice Signs You Are Losing It

Years ago, my aunt and I were traveling to Illinois for the holidays. We were fully loaded with suitcases, two dogs, and assorted gift boxes. While driving, I noticed a number of cars on the side of the road. Because it was cold and potentially icy, I lifted my foot off the accelerator to coast. I noticed my aunt was not wearing her seatbelt, so I encouraged her to strap in. Seeing some "gloss" on the roadway alerted me the roads were likely slippery. Within moments of hearing the clicking of my aunt's seatbelt, my car struck a large patch of black ice. The vehicle swerved side to side. I knew we were in trouble.

My brakes were useless. I clenched the steering wheel, then braced for impact as the car slid toward the side of the highway. We rammed a large pile of snow and bounced onto the highway. The force of the collision thrust my aunt and me forward. Our seatbelts locked up. We spun in circles and came to a stop facing backwards on the highway. All of us, including the dogs, were safe, so we pulled off the highway for a breather. This was intense!

There is nothing fun about black ice. Likewise, there is nothing fun about living with our relational circuits offline or interacting with people who are relationally offline. In this diminished state, relational casualties are inevitable. We have little tolerance for what bothers, annoys, offends, or frustrates us. We are a shadow of the person we are meant to be. It is safe to say we cannot reflect the best of our character when we are in this weakened state!

We must learn to notice the signs that we and others are falling out of relational mode—then make adjustments. If I am going offline, it is time to use a Joy Switch habit. When I see you are going offline, my goal is to stay relational while I interact with you. One of the easiest ways to navigate this terrain is by taking a purposeful pause, a momentary breather, to quiet and rest. This brings us to the third Joy Switch habit, *Rest*.

THE "R" IN *CARS*: REST

In chapter 3, we learned the "C" in *CARS* for *Connection*. In chapter 4, we learned the "A" for *Appreciation*. Now we look at the "R" in *CARS* for *Rest*.

How well we rest is the greatest predictor of lifelong mental health.[6] Rest is also a foundational skill for the success of our brain's relational engine. Deep breathing activates the parasympathetic branch of our nervous system, and this system helps our body rest and relax. We quiet when we take some deep breaths and try to calm down. The pause in my interaction with Mason, the moment of rest, was crucial to help Mason regain his relational circuit. Once we paused together, he could shift into relational mode to find peace, understanding, even a bit of joy.

Rest is an underrated skill. No matter how difficult our circumstances, staying relational requires rest. Rest recharges our relational battery. By far, one of the hardest steps in a difficult interaction is keeping our own relational circuit on while we interact with others who are losing it. All too often, we lose our relational circuit and shift into airplane (enemy) mode because we need a breather, and someone fails to see this and stop. The person who is upset does not notice our need (and theirs) to pause, so they keep talking and reacting. Eventually big emotions become too much and the circuit blows. We go offline. For this reason, we want to take deep breaths and invite others to join us for a relational pause. Rest is the gift that keeps on giving. It is worth noting that even "the silent treatment" from someone we love can be too much and cause our relational circuit to go offline. Too much stimulation can lead to pain. But so can a lack of emotional input.

What happens in you when someone doesn't stop to let you rest?

Rest Is a Fading Skill

During a number of interactions with my wife, in the middle of our conversation, I would break eye contact, pick up my phone, and check email as a distraction. This was often in the middle of an intense discussion. The expression on my wife's face told me this was not increasing her joy levels. Jen's words confirmed it with, "Am I boring you? Why are you picking up your phone right now?"

Sadly, this happened a number of times. I had no clue why I was doing this!

I took some time to reflect, and the thought occurred to me. *I turn to my phone the moment I reach my limit and need a breather.* Instead of using my words to say, "Honey, can we pause this conversation so I can catch my breath?" or something along those lines, I turned to my pseudo-quieting habit—the phone. Once I realized the source of this unwanted behavior, I shared my discovery with Jen. Together, we started to pay closer attention for the signals either of us needs a breather, so we could pause. Our interactions improved.

Of all the relational skills we can learn, rest is one of the hardest to sustain, because our ever-changing world makes it increasingly difficult to rest. We have more to distract us than ever before. Changes in technology increase the likelihood we will plug in to phones, tablets, and screens.[7] We carry around our phones, so any free time is used to check email, search online, shop, text, and interact with others through the small device that fits in a pocket or purse.

Devices hijack our attention. Research shows when we have our phones close to us, even when we are not using the phone, our cognitive capacity is diminished.[8] *Even if the phone is turned off or face down in silent mode, our brain is still thinking about checking our phone.* We may have our phone turned off while we focus on a task, but the phone is still pulling precious bandwidth from our brain. The greater our dependence on the phone, the greater our cognitive decreases will show up, especially if the phone is within reach while we try to focus on another task.[9] Professor Dr. Larry Rosen commented on this research and mentioned students who study with their phones by their side will study for "only ten out of the fifteen minutes, which is their maximum ability to pay attention and not feel compelled to check their phones."[10] Our ability to focus and keep our attention is harder than ever.

If we translate this research to relationships, what it means is we are distracted with shorter attention spans. It means our relational circuit is offline. We are pursuing "pseudo-joys" for joy and artificial means for quieting. Our ability to "cool off" with rest and quiet is negatively impacted. When we fail to rest, we compensate using BEEPS. We rely on BEEPS for comfort, the *Behaviors*, *Experiences*, *Events*, *People*, and *Substances* to artificially regulate our emotions.

Linda Stone came up with the term "Email Apnea" or "Screen Apnea" to describe how we hold our breath or shallow-breathe when we pick up our phones or check email.[11] Stone observed about 80 percent of people she tested had email apnea. Most of the people in the 20 percent who did not hold their breath had some sort of previous breathing training in their history.[12] What do you notice in your body and breathing when you pick up your phone?

As a Family . . .

As a family, we now use the *Rest* habit regularly. Jen and I both take moments to pause and "catch our breath." We ask our sons to take a "Quiet Practice" anytime it is clear their relational engine is offline or they are coasting toward enemy mode.[13] We can identify the need for rest by watching their actions and behaviors, listening to their voice tone, and paying attention to their words. Without this purposeful pause, behaviors inevitably deteriorate to the point they will get into trouble. The quiet practice happens when we see our sons become too hyper, no longer listen, and stop following instructions. Arguing, fighting, and becoming nonrelational in some way are all signs rest is needed to activate the relational circuit. Pressing the pause button recharges us with focus and energy. This Joy Switch is crucial for parents, teachers, coaches, and anyone who interacts with another human being.

Since we started implementing quiet practice as a family, the peace levels in our home have significantly increased. Many parents make the classic mistake of using time-out or isolation in the bedroom as a punishment to modify behaviors. This is not a good substitute for quieting and rest because it creates loss and attachment pain in younger children, which weakens rather than strengthens the relational circuit. Instead, try a relational rest. Make *Rest* the habit your family uses as an opportunity to catch your breath, so you better connect with each other in rhythms of joy and peace. Rest should be the reward and the preventative response for behavior—not the punishment.

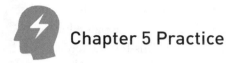 **Chapter 5 Practice**

EXERCISE 11: *RESTFUL BREATHING*

Practice resting to see if you can calm your body and mind. Try to notice changes which take place during and after rest practice. Turn off your phone's ringer and feel free to experiment with relaxing music.

1. First assess whether you are in relational mode. Review the checklist below. If you answer *Yes* to any of these, your relational circuit is offline.

   Simple Enemy Mode

   ☐ I just want to make a problem, person, or feeling go away.

   ☐ I don't want to listen to what others feel or say.

   ☐ My mind is "locked onto" something upsetting.

   ☐ I don't want to be connected to _____. (Someone I usually like.)

   ☐ I just want to get away, or fight, or freeze.

   ☐ I more aggressively interrogate, judge, and fix other people.

2. Next, find a book and a comfortable position where you lie down on your back without supporting any part of your body.

3. Set a timer for three to five minutes then place the book
   on your belly and breathe deeply so you see the book rise
   and fall with each breath.[14]

   a. Inhale through your nose and exhale out your mouth.
   b. It is common for our brain to be busy when we try
      to rest. Some people find it helpful to remember
      peaceful, calming moments.

4. Once you finish, notice your body and observe any changes
   after the quieting practice. Try this sequence several
   times.

5. Now assess once again whether you are in relational
   mode by reviewing the checklist above.

6. Try this exercise two to three times a day and see what
   you notice.

EXERCISE 12: *EXAMPLES FOR RESTING*

We can invite others to take a breather when we notice
people need a pause. The invitation to rest along with examples and stories of times we practiced rest can be refreshing.
Storytelling is a brain-friendly way to demonstrate habits
we want others to learn or practice. For this exercise, personal examples will go a long way.

1. Think about times in your life when you successfully rested. Include answers to the questions below.

   a. How did you quiet yourself? What did you do?
   b. What have you found helpful when you need rest?

2. Next, think of examples where you observed someone calm down and rest. What did this person do in order to rest and quiet?

3. Share these thoughts and stories with a friend or family member.

4. When you finish, invite your listener to share how they rest along with examples of times they rested or observed someone rest.

5. Discuss with your friend or family member what makes resting easy or difficult. Share ideas and solutions for additional practice that can be inserted into your day.

EXERCISE 13: *PRESSING THE PAUSE*[15]

Quieting your body makes it easier to rest and enjoy a *relational Time-Out*. We practice quieting our body and lowering our tension levels. Without enough rest, it will be difficult to stay out of enemy mode.

1. Make yourself comfortable by lying down so you do not need to support any part of your body.

2. Scan your body and notice where you feel muscle tension and stiffness.

3. Take several deep belly breaths then tighten your whole body from the top of your head to the soles of your feet while you slowly count to seven.

4. Next, relax each part of your body, beginning with your forehead, face, neck, shoulders, back, hands, stomach, buttocks, legs, feet, and toes.

5. Try several rounds of tightening your body then loosening your muscles while you take deep belly breaths.

6. Notice how you are feeling and if you have remaining tension. Try this exercise until your body starts to relax.

7. Close with a prayer of gratitude for what you feel thankful for today. You can also type your gratitude in your phone, write in your journal or share with a friend or family member.

SUSTAINING THE SWITCHED-ON LIFE

QUICK TAKE

Learning to sustain the switched-on life is about training our brain to run on joy and use peace as the gauge to alert us when we are in danger of losing our relational circuit. Just as joy is the fuel to sustain the relational circuit, fear is the fuel for airplane (enemy) mode. Fear puts and keeps us in enemy mode. Fear robs our peace. Learning to recognize when we lose our peace is one of the best ways to notice when we have fallen out of relational mode. The Shalom My Body exercises are the final element, the "S" in the *CARS* sequence. These exercises restore peace to our mind and body, which help us stay relational.

FOR OVER A YEAR my younger son asked for a puppy. We deferred our decision as long as we could; then the coronavirus shut the world down. *What better time for a new puppy,* we thought. Several phone calls later, we found our new furball. A fluffy, white, four-pound dog named Bella.

Bella is bright and spunky, full of excitement and energy. Bella is a great gift to our family. Yet somehow, I underestimated the work involved with a new puppy. We needed to train Bella to distinguish inside from outside for bathroom needs. It did not take long before we realized *house training a puppy is essential for sustaining joy levels.* We needed to interpret Bella's cues to tell us when she wanted to go outside. Sleep is short those first few nights of training. I vividly remember the times Jen or I would walk Bella outside, in the rain, so she could do her business. After waiting, to no avail, we bring her inside where she would run to the living room and relieve herself. It was easy for our brain's relational circuit to go offline in those moments.

Most of us can relate to the difficulties associated with those daily irritations that make it hard to stay relational. Sometimes it's the smaller things that make it hard to stay relational, not just the "big-ticket" items. Have you ever had one of those days where several small annoyances began to pile up? Pets, hassles with your tech, waiting on the phone to talk to a real person about your insurance question, spilling your coffee . . . all these things can take away our joy.

Puppies are cute, the source of smiles, cuddles, and

laughter. Yet the lack of house-training means the fun of a new puppy quickly disappears. Without training, even bubbly puppies become an irritation. The relational circuit is a lot like the new puppy who needs training.

JOY, PAIN, AND THE UNTRAINED RELATIONAL CIRCUIT

When trained, the relational circuit is the source of great joy—the secret ingredient behind smiles, connection, warmth, love, belonging, security, resilience. When untrained, the relational circuit becomes the source of pain and relational ruptures. An untrained relational circuit, like an untrained dog, is unpredictable and unreliable. People may attack or pull away from us, leaving loved ones feeling alone and on edge. We lose faith in people who attack when things go wrong—or pull away during hardship and adversity.

Many things meant to be joyful and rewarding quickly become painful because someone's relational circuits are offline. Nowhere is this clearer than in marriage and parenting. The fear of getting hurt by someone's words or actions causes immense pain. It also keeps our own relational circuit offline. Many children live with a parent who is stuck in enemy mode, whose words and actions hurt, whose moods are unpredictable. In many cases, these parents are simply passing on the pain they experienced growing up. Too many unwanted patterns are passed down the family line where parents do not have access to their relational circuits. The result is children who develop fear. Pain is instilled, then passed on. The effects are detrimental to our mental health, and brain research is just now beginning to understand how often these destructive patterns lead to a host of personality disorders. The younger children are when things go wrong, the greater the consequences.[1] To remain our relational selves during times of hardship, we need a trained relational circuit.[2]

An untrained relational circuit means someone does not calm down when big feelings arise. The person in enemy mode fails to protect others from their words and reactions. The nonrelational brain loses its filter, so people say and do hurtful things. Here we see bullying. Being with someone who has an untrained relational circuit is like trying to hug a cactus tree. When you get close, you get pricked.

The quality of brain training determines the quality of relationships we can build. Even though people may not have the language, they intuitively recognize a working relational circuit when it's present—or absent. All it takes is a bit of observation to realize if someone's relational circuit is working. We hear statements like "Be careful, Joe is having one of his bad days!" or "Watch out, Pam woke up on the wrong side of the bed again!"

In truth, words fail to paint an accurate picture of the devastating effects of living with someone in enemy mode. The pain may well last a lifetime. It is heartbreaking.

How Fear Fuels Enemy Mode

As we have seen, families can be devastated by fear, especially of a member whose relational circuit is unreliable, often off. When we are stuck in enemy mode, we are guided by fear—our own and that of others. Enemy mode is our brain's way of avoiding what causes pain. We rely on fear to get results. As Dr. Jim Wilder says in *The Pandora Problem*, it is common for people to avoid speaking up, to correct or criticize an angry or offline person, because they fear the reaction.[3] A narcissist cannot process shame.[4] Because he cannot receive correction or criticism, those around him fear confronting him. Unfortunately, this creates a harmful dynamic where the narcissist is enabled in his toxic behavior because others tiptoe around tough issues and strive to please the shameless one.

We can think about people in our life and categorize who appears to have regular access to their relational circuit and who doesn't. The good news is, when we know how, practice goes a long way to train new puppies and relational circuits.

Let's now look at peace—and its importance in remaining relational.

THE PEACE TEST

What do you do if you think you have a fever? You probably start by feeling your forehead. Next you find a thermometer and take your temperature. Likewise, we need to learn to "take our peace temperature." For the health and status of our relational circuit, the presence of peace is a good indicator the relational circuit is working. The absence of peace alerts us we have a problem. We want to learn to pay attention to our peace levels. As soon as we realize our peace is dropping out, it is time to use the Joy Switch.

How can we tell if we're losing our peace? For many of us, we catch ourselves focusing on a problem. We realize we are holding our breath or tightening our abdominal muscles as though we are bracing for a gut punch. We may get lost on our phones with mindless scrolling. Tension in our shoulders. Trouble focusing on a task. The urge to surrender and give in to a craving. We feel critical and judgmental toward other people. We develop nervous habits like twiddling our hair or thumbs. The list goes on. What do you notice when you lose your peace?

The most important thing is to ask ourselves, "Do I feel peaceful right now?" This is the big question to check if we are relational or slipping into airplane (enemy) mode.

Peace comes when we know we are not alone with our feelings and that *how we feel* makes sense for the situation we face.[5] Peace in Hebrew is *Shalom*, which means everything is in the right relationship, at the right time, in the right place, at the right strength, and in the right amount for God and people.[6] Shalom is the *sweet spot* for our nervous system, our relationships with people, and our relationship with God. Staying in the sweet spot largely depends on the status of the relational circuit.

One practical way to check peace levels is to notice our breathing. Are you breathing deeply and feeling relaxed, or tense and tight? With some effort, we can notice the presence or absence of peace. Peace is the litmus test, the fuel gauge, for our brain's relational engine. Below is a *PEACE Check* to assess peace levels. Review the list and see what you notice.

PEACE Check
Pay attention to my body
Evaluate my breathing
Attention and focus
Calm or busy thoughts
Easing muscle tension

Pay attention to my body:

☐ *My body feels calm, content, and relaxed.*
☐ *My body feels strained, tense, and uptight.*

Evaluate my breathing:

☐ *My breathing is deep and relaxed from my belly.*
☐ *My breathing is shallow and tense from my chest.*

Attention and focus:

☐ *I notice my focus is on positive and peaceful things, which relaxes me.*

☐ *I notice my focus is on problems. I replay scenes of upsetting moments, conversations, and interactions. I focus on pain, trying to avoid pain or make pain stop.*

Calm or busy thoughts:

☐ *My thoughts are peaceful as I reflect on the things and people for which I feel thankful.*

☐ *My thoughts are racing. Busy thoughts focus on the things or people which make me angry, afraid, hurt, etc.*

Easing muscle tension:

☐ *My muscles feel loose, rested, and content.*

☐ *My body feels tense, anxious, and strained.*

The body is the canvas for the brain, so learning to pay attention to our body tells us a lot about how our brain is doing. What story is your body telling you? This short PEACE check helps us notice our body to see how our relational circuit is holding up. This brings us to our next Joy Switch step, the "S" in *CARS*, which stands for Shalom My Body.

HITTING THE SWEET SPOT!

I enjoyed playing baseball growing up. Each time I stepped to the plate with my bat, I had one goal: *hit the ball*. I didn't care if I hit a home run, a double, or a single. My primary goal was to reach the base and avoid striking out.

Every now and then I would hit the ball in just the right way, where it felt like perfection to make contact. This "perfection" was known as the *sweet spot* on the bat, the "meat" in the bat where the ball would bounce fast and travel far.

One time I was playing in a city tournament, and the opposing pitcher was a star athlete who could throw a fastball few batters could hit. My team struggled to hit the ball. We were embarrassed by how well this guy's pitching was dominating us. As the game began to wind down, my friend John stepped to the plate. At this point, we didn't care about winning or losing. We simply wanted some dignity restored by hitting the ball.

John took his position at the plate. The pitcher wound up, then threw one of his fastballs. John stunned everyone by hitting the ball with the sweet part of the bat. I knew by the crack of the bat that this was special. The ball easily sailed over the centerfield fence for a home run. The bench cleared. We stormed the field to celebrate John. Even the pitcher looked surprised to see someone hit his fastball.

After the game, I pulled John aside and asked him a burning question. "John, how did you do it? How did you hit the ball so far?" John paused for a moment, then said, "I closed my eyes and swung the bat." He must have noticed my jaw dropping, so he continued, "Much to my surprise, I hit the ball, and it went over the fence!"

We both laughed in astonishment. John hit a home run with closed eyes. Without realizing it, John hit the ball in the sweet spot of his bat and saved the day by scoring a run.

We all want to live our best life with the time we have left. We want to stay in our relational sweet spot. Here we become the most relationally engaged, joyful people we can be. Living in the sweet spot is not so much about luck, as it was for John. Staying in the sweet spot is more about *practice*. John swung the bat hundreds, even thousands of times before he hit a home run that day. John always dreamed about hitting a home run to win the big game. Even with closed eyes, John accomplished his dream.

Practice pays off when we rehearse important habits needed for relationships. Imagine the possibilities when you stay relational and hold onto your peace.

THE "S" IN *CARS*: SHALOM MY BODY

We now know one of the first signs our relational circuit is diminishing is the *absence of peace*. When peace goes away, something else fills the void. We may feel high-energy emotions increase, such as anger and fear. Or we may have low-energy shame, disgust, or hopeless despair. Big emotions we cannot handle will inevitably turn off the relational circuit. With practice, we learn to notice the first signs our peace is fading; then we return to a peaceful state.[7] The goal is to reach shalom for our mind and body. Losing our peace is the warning shot alerting us it is time to correct course.

One practical way to infuse shalom into our life is by practicing useful exercises my colleagues call Shalom My

Body.[8] Here we practice the Shalom My Body exercises to calm our body and lessen the stress response.[9] These exercises are designed to stimulate the vagal nerve, which is the main parasympathetic nerve in our body, known as the "brakes," or the "Rest and Digest" response we rely on to calm high-energy reactions.[10] The vagal nerve is known as the "wandering nerve" because it spreads throughout the body and stimulates muscles in the heart to slow down our heart rate so we calm down. While this nerve has several important roles in the body, we can practice specific exercises[11] to stimulate the vagal nerve, which help us calm and regain access to our relational circuit. If the light of our relational engine starts to dim, we can use *Shalom* exercises to feel clearer, more grounded, and peaceful.

The Shalom My Body exercises reduce the body's stress response. Trying the steps may feel strange at first. There are three specific exercises. One exercise may be more effective than the others, so try some experimentation and see what you notice. The exercises at the end of this chapter provide opportunity to practice each step. The three exercises are:[12]

Shalom Sequence #1—*Yawn Left and Yawn Right*
Shalom Sequence #2—*Breathe and Scrunch*
Shalom Sequence #3—*Knock to Wake Up Your Attachment Center*

Once you notice an improvement in how you feel when you return to relational mode, your brain will *want to do it again*. Anything that helps you feel better and conserves energy by spending less time in enemy mode is a step in the right direction. The Shalom My Body exercises shorten the relational-circuit gap so we better bounce back to relational mode.[13]

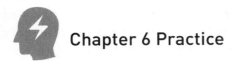

Chapter 6 Practice

EXERCISE 14: *SHALOM MY BODY*

We have worked our way through the *CARS* habits to the final letter, *S* for *Shalom My Body*. First you assess the status of your relational circuit, then use your phone or computer to view the demonstration exercises. Practice each exercise. Once you finish, check your relational circuit status and notice how you feel.

1. Check whether you are in relational mode. Review the checklist below. If you answer *Yes* to any of these, your relational circuit is offline.

   Simple Enemy Mode
   - ☐ I just want to make a problem, person, or feeling go away.
   - ☐ I don't want to listen to what others feel or say.
   - ☐ My mind is "locked onto" something upsetting.
   - ☐ I don't want to be connected to _____.
     (Someone I usually like.)
   - ☐ I just want to get away, or fight, or freeze.
   - ☐ I more aggressively interrogate, judge, and fix other people.

2. Visit the YouTube channel Chris Coursey – THRIVEtoday to view the Shalom My Body exercises. Try the exercises, and if your relational circuit is off, you should notice an increase in peace and relational alertness. If you are already relational, you may not notice a dramatic shift, however, you should feel peaceful.

3. Review whether you are in relational mode, and check if anything changed. If you answer *Yes* to any of the above identifiers, your relational circuit is still offline.

4. The goal is to try several rounds of these exercises during moments you feel relationally offline. It is the transitioning from enemy mode back to relational mode that helps your brain learn the value of the Shalom My Body exercises.

EXERCISE 15: *ADDITIONAL SIGNS MY RELATIONAL CIRCUIT IS ON OR OFF*

The Joy Switch introduces signs your relational circuit is on or off, but there are numerous indicators that show you are in relational mode or enemy mode. Here are a few more for you to review. See if you can find additional signs you and others are in relational or enemy mode.

1. *Focus:*

   a. ON: I normally think about the good stuff. I find positive traits in other people and good stuff in my day.

b. OFF: I feel critical. I focus on what's wrong. I look for what feels threatening or frustrating. My singular focus is on something to fix or avoid.

c. What else do you notice with your focus when you are relationally online or offline?

2. *Flexibility:*

a. ON: I easily adjust my expectations and recover from disappointment. People think I am easy-going much of the time.

b. OFF: I feel rigid. People may think I am driven. I do not recover from disappointment. I may feel animosity toward others when I do not get my way. I become punitive in my responses. I punish people for their mistakes. I hold grudges. I may be stuck thinking about what frustrates me.

c. What else do you notice as it relates to flexibility when you are relationally online or offline?

3. *Updating:*

a. ON: I can update my mind with new information once it's presented to me.

b. OFF: I cannot update my mind even when new information is presented. I stay stuck in my feelings and opinions. There is no reasoning with me.

c. What else do you notice in your ability to update when you are relationally online or offline?

4. *Teachable:*

   a. ON: I am receptive to instructions. I can receive correction. I feel like I can learn from anyone; people would say I am teachable.

   b. OFF: I cannot receive or learn something new. Nor do I want to. I feel threatened or insulted when people try to tell me something I already know. I justify my responses. I am judgmental toward others.[14]

   c. What else do you notice as it relates to your ability to stay teachable when you are relationally online or offline?

5. What additional signs can you think of when you fall into enemy mode? Invite family and friends to share observations they see when you are relational—or when you have slipped into enemy mode.

   a. Example: *Loved ones may see changes in your voice tone or your body language. The look on your face tells them you are in enemy mode.*

STARTING A RELATIONAL REVIVAL

QUICK TAKE

Learning to use the Joy Switch to stay relational in our spiritual life has the potential to transform our lives. It is common for many of us to approach our spiritual life stuck in airplane (enemy) mode. When we seek to interact with God *when we are in enemy mode*, God will inevitably feel distant. We will feel relationally disconnected. When we first seek God's peace from a relational place, we start our prayer times thinking about all that is good instead of starting with the focus on pain and problems. This subtle shift in sequence leads to peace and joyful connection. The Bible would say it this way: "Do not be anxious about anything, but in every situation, by prayer and petition, with thanksgiving, present your requests to God. And the peace of God, which transcends all understanding, will guard your hearts and your minds in Christ Jesus" (Phil. 4:6–7). Starting with thanksgiving and gratitude leads to God's peace.

OF ALL THE AREAS touched by the relational circuit, few are as noticeable as *spirituality*. Our spiritual life has potential to reach new heights when we engage the relational circuit and minimize the effects of enemy mode. Staying relational during prayer times, fellowship, worship, even spiritual disciplines, sharpen our spiritual eyes and heighten our spiritual ears to better sense and enjoy God's peace. It also reduces the "noise" that distracts us from finding that peace. Everything about our spiritual walk is improved when we learn to stay in our sweet spot.

What keeps us from feeling God's peace? Often, it's because *the relational circuit goes offline* when we approach our time with God. Once our relational brain shifts to enemy mode with God, we lose all ability to joyfully interact with another relational being. Like trying to see with our eyes closed, we feel disconnected. Approaching God when we are in enemy mode is an excellent way to ensure God *feels* distant because our brain is in the worst possible position for a relational interaction.

There is another way.

If we struggle to stay relational with God, it may be because we lack the training to feel appreciation. Or perhaps we have painful difficulties that arise when we think about God or consider connecting with His peace. Or we might relate to Gianna—who believed God had given up on her.

"GOD DOESN'T SPEAK WITH ME!"

A few years ago, I was leading a training event, and the staff asked if I would meet with someone during an afternoon break. I agreed. I later found out a few more details about the person I was meeting. Her name was Gianna, and she had given up. She also felt like God abandoned her. Gianna's life was in shambles. She felt hopeless. Gianna reached out in desperation, her last-ditch effort to see if someone could help.

I walked into the office, and Gianna was sitting on the couch. She turned to me and said, "This is a waste of your time, because God doesn't speak with me!" I knew right then this meeting would require a fully functioning relational circuit—for both of us!

Gianna continued. "For forty years I have tried everything to find God. He is nowhere to be found. He must hate me!" My first observation was Gianna's relational circuit was offline. This meant my goal was to gently help Gianna access her brain's relational engine using the Joy Switch.

I started with the first Joy Switch step, the C in *CARS*

to *Connect*. I validated Gianna in the big emotions she was feeling. I said, "Gianna, I can't imagine how hard your journey has been for you! This sounds awful. I am glad I can be here with you." She looked skeptical. After more attunement, I shifted to the *A* in *CARS* for *Appreciation*. I asked, "Is there anything in your life that is good right now, or positive? Anything that brings you joy?" Gianna's immediate response: "No."

But then she said, "Wait. I have one thing."

Now I was curious. Gianna continued. "I have a foster child who is my *everything*." I noticed a sparkle in Gianna's eyes. Her face lit up when she mentioned the foster child. Here was the spark of joy I was looking for. I followed this statement with, "Please, tell me more!"

After several moments listening to Gianna discuss her foster child, I could see her relational circuit was brightly shining. I said, "Okay, I know you feel God has given up on you. But I suspect your pain is 'loud,' which makes it hard to find God's peace. Would you feel comfortable with me praying for you?" By this point, Gianna was in relational mode. I sensed the time was right to pause and look for God's peaceful presence. Gianna said, "Well, if you say so. I don't care if you pray." Here was the openness I was looking for.

I prayed, and at the end, I asked God if there was something peaceful He wanted to share with Gianna. I invited Gianna to look for peace. After several moments of silence, I looked up and noticed tears streaming down her cheeks. I waited until Gianna opened her eyes. She said, "Well, that was strange!" I asked what happened. Gianna responded with, "Well, I don't know if this is God, but the thought that came to my mind was, 'God feels for me what I feel for my foster child.'"

"Hmm. Is this something you think God would say?" I asked.

"I *think* so," said Gianna. We tested her thoughts with the PEACE test, as well as verses in the Bible about God's character. And she said, smiling, "Yes, this thought brings me great peace. I think this might be a gift from God!" By the end of our short meeting, Gianna felt like she enjoyed a peaceful moment with God *for the first time in her life*.

I later found out Gianna's life turned around in some remarkable ways. She now smiles at people. She is involved in several groups at church. This was all new for Gianna, whose life was touched with God's peace. A little of that peace went a long way for Gianna, who simply needed some practice staying relational.

PURSUING GOD'S PEACE

Over the years, my colleagues and I have trained thousands of people around the globe to learn how to be relational in their spiritual life, with remarkable results.[1] There is nothing special or magical about the process with Gianna. *My goal was to help Gianna use the Joy Switch to start her brain's relational engine.* The shift would help Gianna change her focus from what is wrong or painful (airplane/enemy mode) to something uplifting (relational mode). This shift would increase her capacity to better navigate the hard stuff. Maybe she would even feel God's peace in the middle of it all!

The process of getting relational and finding God's signature, which is peace,[2] is about us finding our *ideal relational sweet spot* so we can enjoy God's peaceful presence. For most people, their greatest obstacle to enjoying God's peace is staying relational long enough to notice. This means we must practice and improve our ability to think about and feel appreciation. Trying to force a moment with God only activates enemy mode because the pressure knocks us out of relational mode as fears pop up. If peace is God's signature, then fear is the weed that grows when peace is missing. Fears can arise when I fear God will not answer my prayers. Or I will feel like a failure if nothing happens when I look for God's peace. Or possibly God *will* answer and what will He say to me? Even this can be intimidating for people who fear God's wrath, disappointment, or rejection.

I do not think God is a gumball machine, something we can manipulate by dropping our quarter into the slot and expecting bubblegum to drop out. The process of getting relational does not ensure we will have an awareness of God's peace. *This peaceful awareness is a byproduct of staying relational with God.* The benefits of getting and staying relational in our spiritual life are:

1. This state is the best reflection of who we are meant to be.
2. This state is where we are in the best position to notice and feel peace.
3. This state is where we notice God's peaceful presence *as a reflection of the goodness of God*, who brings sunshine and rain whether or not we deserve it.[3]

Getting relational with God means there is a chance we will find God's peace. If not, the worst thing to happen is we become more relationally engaged. The best thing is, we will enjoy God's peace that shapes our thoughts and molds our character.[4]

STUCK IN ENEMY MODE WITH GOD

For many people who struggle with God's peace, thinking about God stimulates two common responses. First, reflecting on God activates all the negative "files" we have experienced as it relates to our perception of God, God's Word, or God's people. Here, pockets of pain from negative experiences are activated. Once pain is present, our brain shifts into enemy mode. *Thinking about pain and hurts is a great way to remain in nonrelational mode with people and with God.* This means any thoughts or conversations around God trigger our pain, and the result is we are stuck, upset, and nonrelational.

This was the case with Gianna, who was stuck in abandonment pain with God. She didn't need me to discuss theology. First and foremost, Gianna needed the Joy Switch to find her relational circuit. This approach can be seen in the Psalms where the psalmist is in some kind of distress. In the midst of his suffering, the psalmist remembers previous times spent with God's peace. By the end of the Psalm, the writer is praising and thanking God *even though he is still in the same circumstances.*[5]

The second response to thinking about God involves approaching Him with a laser-sharp focus on our needs, our problems, our hurts, our fears and pretty much anything that robs *our* peace. We turn to God with a grocery list of items we want Him to fix, problems we want solved, or hurts we want healed. There is absolutely nothing wrong with turning to God with our needs and hurts! In fact, this is something we are encouraged to do in the Bible.[6] Asking God for help, perspective, and comfort is a normal part of a relationship with the God who owns the cattle on a thousand hills.[7] However, as it relates to our relational circuit, any time we focus on what's wrong, we put ourselves in an ideal position to *remain in enemy mode*. In enemy mode, we quickly feel alone and disconnected. Many among the faithful feel like they must "white knuckle" their faith. This means we keep looking for God, even though we have no peace or even any idea whether God truly sees, hears, or understands.

Here is why many give up on God. People feel God

has abandoned them during their most painful times. It is when our relational circuit is activated that we can discover the gold hidden in our pain.

I propose we turn to God with our thanksgiving and appreciation as a first step, which puts us in our ideal state of a fully engaged relational circuit.[8] In relational mode, we can share minds with God to express our grievances, share our hurts, find His perspective, and receive His comfort.[9] Here is where we find God's peace. One approach keeps us in enemy mode where we amplify pain and feel isolated. The other puts us in our ideal state to receive and relationally interact until we feel peaceful and hopeful. Which do you prefer?

RELATIONAL PRAYER FOR PAIN

Even though I grew up attending a small church in central Illinois where I learned about God and the Bible, learning to stay relational and find God's peace was a brand-new concept for me later in life. It never occurred to me I could enjoy God's peace!

I found relational times with God especially meaningful during the season I injured my back while working on a ladder. Over time, my back injury turned into chronic pain that robbed my sleep, disrupted my workday, and worst of all, limited my ability to play with my young sons. This was a lot of loss, and back pain makes staying relational difficult.

As weeks turned to months, discouragement crept in.

Despite seeing numerous physicians for relief, my back condition worsened. One day, while sitting in a recliner looking out the window to my backyard, I noticed all the trees were bare. All signs of life, the green and color, was gone. Trees and grass were brown. Because this was winter in central Illinois, I was not surprised by the scene. However, I was surprised by this nagging thought: *I wonder if God is done with me.* In this moment, I felt my life had dried up.

I recognized my peace was gone and hopeless despair was present. I knew my brain was plunging into enemy mode as I focused on pain and problems. I paused to get relational. I practiced a Joy Switch step, which was *Appreciation,* from the *CARS* sequence. I first remembered gifts in my life, then I shifted to other times I felt God's peace. This warmed up my relational circuit. I said a prayer, something like:

"Lord, this is how I feel right now. Everything is bare. There is no life growing in me. I feel neglected and hopeless. My back is robbing me."

I then asked God a question:

"What is on Your mind for me? Is there something You want me to know or see from Your perspective?"

After a few moments of using the *Rest* Joy Switch habit, I sensed Jesus sitting next to me, which brought peace. Several thoughts came to mind:

"Chris, what you see is death. What I see is an opportunity

for My life to be revealed. Keep looking out the window . . ."

Realizing God's peace was with me brought immense comfort. I was intrigued by the idea God sees something different than I see. I leaned into these thoughts and reflected on God's peace. I continued looking out the window and shared a few more thoughts in prayer:

"But God, I am looking out this window. All I see is emptiness. Nothing. This is how I feel . . ."

As soon as I spoke those words, I watched several birds flutter from tree branches. I did not notice those birds before. Then, I observed squirrels playing deeper in the woods. *There was life in these woods!* I thought to myself. All I needed to do was keep looking. A few more thoughts came to mind.

"It is through weakness My strength is made perfect.[10] One day the dry woods will be teeming with life. Though you can't see it, there is grass, flowers, and plants hidden beneath the ground cover waiting to burst forth at the right time. Though you can't see it, those woods are filled with life just waiting to blossom."

As I thought about these thoughts and their significance, they were no longer about the woods. My life had meaning, even my pain. I felt a sense of purpose. *One day my back pain would no longer define me. One day, this hidden life within me will blossom.* I was feeling hopeful, encouraged, even inspired. I felt more peace. I knew my relational circuit was engaged. I shared the story with Jen.

By then, I felt like God's peace was with me, whispering in my ear. These thoughts were similar to my thoughts, yet they were different. These thoughts were infused with peace even though nothing changed about my circumstances or my back pain.

There was nothing magical about this prayer time. I was simply practicing *relational interactions with God while searching for peace.* When we use the Joy Switch in our times with God, we focus on *staying relationally engaged.* This means inserting the *CARS* sequence into our prayer times. We search for closeness and peace with God. The goal is to stay relational as we enter our time of prayer, praise, Bible study, worship, any form of spiritual activity. God will meet us there.

Chapter 7 Practice

EXERCISE 16: *GROWING GOOD STUFF*

1. Write down five to seven things from your day that were good, meaningful, and joyful.

   a. When you finish writing your list in your phone or journal, notice how your body feels.

2. Write down five to seven gifts in your life for which you feel thankful.

   a. When you finish writing your list in your phone or journal, notice how your body feels.

3. Write down five to seven qualities you appreciate about God's character or presence.

   a. When you finish writing your list in your phone or journal, notice how your body feels.

4. Practice noticing God's peace by thanking God for His gifts and goodness.

5. Review whether you are in relational mode. Keep in mind if you answer *Yes* to any of these, your relational circuit is off.

Simple Enemy Mode

- ☐ I just want to make a problem, person, or feeling go away.
- ☐ I don't want to listen to what others feel or say.
- ☐ My mind is "locked onto" something upsetting.
- ☐ I don't want to be connected to _____. (Someone I usually like.)
- ☐ I just want to get away, or fight, or freeze.
- ☐ I more aggressively interrogate, judge, and fix other people.

6. Try this exercise every day for two weeks and see what you notice with your relational circuit.

EXERCISE 17: *PEOPLE I ENJOY*

1. Make a list of three or four people you feel thankful for.

   a. Write at least three qualities you enjoy about each person.

2. Call each person or send a card or text to express these qualities. It's much better for your relational circuit (and theirs) if you express these qualities in person!

3. Notice how you feel thinking about these "gifts" and focusing on the qualities you enjoy about each person.

4. Throughout this process, check to see if you are in relational mode. Keep in mind if you answer *Yes* to any of these, your relational circuit is off.

Simple Enemy Mode

☐ I just want to make a problem, person, or feeling go away.

☐ I don't want to listen to what others feel or say.

☐ My mind is "locked onto" something upsetting.

☐ I don't want to be connected to _____. (Someone I usually like.)

☐ I just want to get away, or fight, or freeze.

☐ I more aggressively interrogate, judge, and fix other people.

EXERCISE 18: *FINDING GOD'S PEACE*

Enjoying God's peace comes down to our ability to enter into appreciation and stay relational. Any time our brain shifts into enemy mode, it is often because *we need training to stay in appreciation*, or *we have unprocessed pain* that needs attention. Unprocessed pain can show up as fears, immaturity, cravings, broken relationships, and more.

1. After reading this chapter, what comes to your mind when you think about possible obstacles that may hinder you from staying relational with God?

2. Our brain focuses on the things that are the "loudest" or most painful. This makes pain, fear, conflicts, and problems the noisy distractions! When we focus on the loud stuff, it is hard to stay relational and peaceful. This means it's hard to enjoy God's peace. Therefore, we want to train our brain to focus on the good things like appreciation and joy.

   a. Start an appreciation journal to write down five things from your day you feel thankful for before bed each night.

   b. Consider trying the thirty-day appreciation exercise where you practice appreciation three times a day for five minutes each session for thirty days to reset your nervous system for joy and peace. This means focusing on and feeling appreciation for five minutes at a time by reviewing appreciation memories. Try this exercise for thirty days to see what you notice.

3. What comes to mind when you think about closeness with God? This may be positive or negative.

4. Have you ever enjoyed a moment in your life where you felt like God's peace was with you?

   a. If so, turn this into a story you can share with someone.

5. If you cannot think of a moment in your life where you felt like God's peace was with you, practice remembering times you felt like God gave you gifts to enjoy. Notice how appreciation feels.

   a. This would be a good habit to practice on a daily basis.

EXERCISE 19: *BE STILL, NOW MOVE*

Some people feel closer to God's peace during low-energy times that include a quiet place to rest, a comfortable chair, soft music, a cup of coffee or tea, and a journal. Others prefer high-energy movement such as a run, brisk walk, bike ride, or an aerobic exercise to get their body moving. Once moving, they feel closer to God's peace. Here we want to try both methods to compare what we notice as we look for God's peace.[11]

1. Try a high-energy activity like walking, exercising, or jogging. Notice if you feel relational during your outing. As you move, reflect on your favorite memories with:

   a. Family and friends
   b. Traveling spots
   c. Foods and shared meals
   d. Fun activities
   e. Nature, pets, and animals

2. Try a low-energy activity like sitting down, lying on your back, or reclining. As you rest, take some time to reflect on your favorite memories with:

   a. Family and friends
   b. Traveling spots
   c. Foods and shared meals
   d. Fun activities
   e. Nature, pets, and animals

3. What do you notice with each method? Do you prefer one over the other?

LOOKING AHEAD
TO REAL LIFE...

Congratulations! You completed *The Joy Switch*. How well you apply these concepts comes down to *practice*. I encourage you to practice the Joy Switch in your life—a lot!

Momentum increases when people join us on our journey. Family members or friends who walk with you as you put these habits into practice provide much-needed support. Share what you are learning with people in your network. Invite others to read the book then practice the Joy Switch habits with you. Observe how good it feels when you are relational—or how stressful when you are stuck in enemy mode. Noticing and practicing relational habits is the start of something good.

You, my friend, can maximize your full relational potential by living the switched-on life!

ACKNOWLEDGMENTS

Writing *The Joy Switch* turned into an unexpected adventure. Originally, this book was to be written at a later date, but the opportunity arose to write this resource sooner with an earlier release date. About the time I sat down to type my very first words, the coronavirus epidemic struck, virtually shutting down the world. My sons were home from school. My scheduled travels were canceled. Along with the coronavirus, a number of additional challenges soon followed that felt like a "perfect storm." Trying to creatively write a book about staying relational with so much happening at one time sure felt like a steep challenge!

Thankfully, there was a silver lining to the hardship during the writing of this book. I found many opportunities to practice *The Joy Switch* in my life. My family and I practiced staying relational and returning to relational mode throughout the coronavirus quarantine. Basically, I lived this book while I was writing it!

You, the reader, directly benefit from this experience. The challenges in my life provided the framework for much of the content and exercises. I wrote with integrity because I practiced *The Joy Switch* habits, which sharpened the material with each new day.

There are some special people I want to mention who helped make this project happen.

First, I would like to thank my amazing wife, Jen Coursey, for holding down the fort so I could focus on writing this book. Without Jen's contributions and insights, this book would not be here. I wish to thank my wise friend Dr. Jim Wilder for his guidance and oversight. It is because of Jim's work I can write a book like this! Kitty Wilder, Jim's wife, was instrumental in going through this material with Jim. I am deeply appreciative for the help from my creative friend Dr. Marcus Warner, who helped me with the outline for this book.

I am standing on the shoulders of several "tall trees" in the forest, pioneers who have gone before me and laid the foundation so *The Joy Switch* can exist. The priceless work of Dr. Jim Wilder and Dr. Karl Lehman is where this started for me. I am indebted to these two forerunners, and also Charlotte Lehman, Ed and Maritza Khouri, Dr. Marcus Warner, Amy Brown, and all the amazing minds who have invested countless hours to share this treasure with the world.

The reason *The Joy Switch* happened in the first place was because of a lunch conversation with Zack Williamson and Duane Sherman, who came up with the idea a book like this was needed. Everything grew from this lunch meeting, so thank you, Zack and Duane, for being the spark to light this fire!

And Duane, I also deeply appreciate your encouragement, creativity, and wise counsel along the way. As well, I'm grateful for all the wonderful guidance, feedback, and editing work from Betsey Newenhuyse. Thank you, Duane and Betsey, for your incredible help!

I am grateful for the review and support from Lieza Bates, Amy Brown, and Bonnie Wunderly. Many thanks to Kristy Harrang for helping me free my schedule to write this book.

ABOUT THRIVETODAY

THRIVEtoday is a nonprofit organization focused on equipping people with the nineteen relational skills that make relationships work. THRIVEtoday offers a variety of interactive training events to train individuals and groups in relational skills.

THRIVEtoday creates resources, online courses, and materials to give practical steps for people to increase emotional capacity and gain missing skills. THRIVEtoday offers webinars and online events so people learn more about relational skills.

Organizations around the world are now using relational skills to bolster growth and further recovery. This book offers a taste of the nineteen relational skills. To go deeper into the skills, consider attending an event or utilizing one of many resources to get started. If you would like to host Chris or a representative from THRIVEtoday to speak and/or lead a weekend training event for your community, contact us at info@thrivetoday.org.

Learn more about relational skill resources at www.thrivetoday.org.

ABOUT THE AUTHOR

For over twenty years, Chris has been creating and practicing brain-based solutions to make relationships work. Chris enjoys spending time with his wife, Jen, and their two sons in western Michigan. In addition to building joy on the home front, Chris spends most of his time teaching, training, developing materials, fostering relationships, jogging along Lake Michigan, and equipping people to mature, so they live according to their faith and values.

Chris is a published author with nine books in print, including *The 4 Habits of Joy-Filled Marriages*, coauthored with Dr. Marcus Warner. Chris travels the world equipping leaders, families, and communities in relational brain skills.

Notes

Introduction

1. Learn more about the work of Dr. Jim Wilder and the Life Model for transformation at lifemodelworks.org.

2. This circuit goes by many names. The *control center* in Life Model literature (lifemodelworks.org), Dr. Karl Lehman (immanuel approach.com) refers to the brain's control center as the *relational circuitry* in Karl Lehman, *Outsmarting Yourself: Catching Your Past Invading the Present and What to Do about It* (Libertyville, IL: This JOY! Books, 2011), the *fast-track system* by Marcus Warner and E. James Wilder, *RARE Leadership: 4 Uncommon Habits for Increasing Trust, Joy, and Engagement in the People You Lead* (Chicago: Moody Publishers, 2016), the *On/Off switch* in Marcus Warner and Chris Coursey, *The 4 Habits of Joy-Filled Marriages: How 15 Minutes a Day Will Help You Stay in Love* (Chicago: Moody Publishers, 2019); the work of Dr. Allan Schore out of UCLA (allanschore.com) goes into great detail on the role and function of this brain system.

3. The teachings of Dr. Jim Wilder in the THRIVE-at-Home course (thrivetoday.org) and Dr. Karl Lehman (immanuelapproach.com) apply the research of Dr. Allan Schore from UCLA (allanschore .com) on the levels that make up the relational circuitry.

4. Brain plasticity refers to the brain's ability to change over time and rewire itself for new skills and to regain lost or impaired abilities.

Chapter 1: Firing Up Your Relational Circuit

1. I use a version of this story in Chris Coursey, *Transforming Fellowship: 19 Brain Skills That Build Joyful Community* (Holland, MI: Coursey Creations, LLC, 2016), 129–31.

2. This is a fictitious name and elements of this story have been altered to protect Mason's identity.

3. The vast writings and works of Dr. Allan Schore (allanschore.com) discuss this right hemispheric brain system, while Dr. Jim Wilder (lifemodelworks.org) applies this research.

4. Dr. Jim Wilder came up with this terminology as part of the Life Model curriculum. *Acting Like Yourself* is Skill 12 in the THRIVEtoday list of nineteen relational skills (thrivetoday.org).

5. Those who rely on the Bible for guidance can refer to Ephesians 2:10 on how acting like ourselves produces "good works," which are *the result* of being who we were created to be.

6. The writings and teachings of Dr. Jim Wilder (lifemodelworks.org) apply the research of Dr. Allan Schore (allanschore.com) on relational joy.

7. The work and research of Dr. Allan Schore (allanschore.com). More about joy can be found in Life Model materials (lifemodelworks .org) including E. James Wilder, Ed Khouri, Chris. M. Coursey, Shelia D. Sutton, *Joy Starts Here: The Transformation Zone* (East Peoria, IL: Shepherd's House, Inc., 2013).

8. Learn more about joy and the brain's fast-track and slow-track processor in Marcus Warner and E. James Wilder, *RARE Leadership: 4 Uncommon Habits for Increasing Trust, Joy, and Engagement in the People You Lead* (Chicago: Moody Publishers, 2016).

9. Learn about these capacities in the following two books: Chris Coursey, *Transforming Fellowship*; Amy Brown and Chris Coursey, *Relational Skills in the Bible: A Bible Study Focused on Relationships* (Carmel, IN: Deeper Walk International, 2019).

10. E. James Wilder, *The Pandora Problem: Facing Narcissism in Leaders & Ourselves* (Carmel, IN: Deeper Walk International, 2018).

11. Michel Hendricks and E. James Wilder, *The Other Half of Church: Christian Community, Brain Science, and Overcoming Spiritual Stagnation* (Chicago: Moody Publishers, 2020).

12. Visit thrivetoday.org to see the nineteen relational skills.

13. Learn more with Wilder, *The Pandora Problem*.

14. Wilder et al., *Joy Starts Here: The Transformation Zone*.

15. Marcus Warner and Chris Coursey, *The 4 Habits of Joy-Filled Marriages: How 15 Minutes a Day Will Help You Stay in Love* (Chicago: Moody Publishers, 2019).

16. Wilder et al., *Joy Starts Here: The Transformation Zone*.

17. Ibid.

18. Stephanie Hinman and Marcus Warner, *Building Bounce: How to Grow Emotional Resilience* (Carmel, IN: Deeper Walk International, 2020).

Chapter 2: Offline: Recognizing a Shutdown

1. Learn more about these levels with the teachings of Dr. Jim Wilder in the THRIVE-at-Home curriculum (thrivetoday.org), the work of Dr. Karl Lehman (immanuelapproach.com), and Marcus Warner and E. James Wilder, *RARE Leadership: 4 Uncommon Habits for Increasing Trust, Joy, and Engagement in the People You Lead* (Chicago: Moody Publishers, 2016).

2. Term used by Dr. Jim Wilder.

3. I talk more about the role of nonverbal stories in Coursey, *Transforming Fellowship*, 139–47.

4. Marcus Warner and Chris Coursey, *The 4 Habits of Joy-Filled Marriages: How 15 Minutes a Day Will Help You Stay in Love* (Chicago: Moody Publishers, 2019).

5. Dr. Jim Wilder is the source of the different versions and terms of Enemy Mode. Learn more with Michel Hendricks and E. James Wilder, *The Other Half of Church: Christian Community, Brain Science, and Overcoming Spiritual Stagnation* (Chicago: Moody Publishers, 2020) and E. James Wilder, *The Pandora Problem: Facing Narcissism in Leaders & Ourselves* (Carmel, IN: Deeper Walk International, 2018).

6. Hendricks and Wilder, *The Other Half of Church*, 88.

7. Adapted from the *Belonging* module in the Connexus program designed by Ed Khouri (equippinghearts.com) and Dr. Jim Wilder (lifemodelworks.org) and the book *Outsmarting Yourself: Catching Your Past Invading the Present and What to Do about It* (Libertyville, IL: This JOY! Books, 2011) by Karl Lehman.

8. For an in-depth look at relational circuits in the ON or OFF position, review Lehman, *Outsmarting Yourself* and Khouri and Wilder, *Belonging* in the Connexus program.

9. Hendricks and Wilder, *The Other Half of Church*, 88.

10. Ibid.

11. This point is from the work and writings of Dr. Jim Wilder.

Chapter 3: Get Back on Track!

1. Wilder et al., *Joy Starts Here: The Transformation Zone* (East Peoria, IL: Shepherd's House, Inc., 2013).

2. I recommend the VCR process for attunement. Learn more with Marcus Warner and E. James Wilder, *RARE Leadership: 4 Uncom-*

mon Habits for Increasing Trust, Joy, and Engagement in the People You Lead (Chicago: Moody Publishers, 2016). Also, Marcus Warner and Chris Coursey, *The 4 Habits of Joy-Filled Marriages: How 15 Minutes a Day Will Help You Stay in Love* (Chicago: Moody Publishers, 2019).

3. Learn more about attunement with Karl Lehman, *Outsmarting Yourself: Catching Your Past Invading the Present and What to Do about It* (Libertyville, IL: This JOY! Books, 2011); Warner and Wilder, *RARE Leadership*; Warner and Coursey, *The 4 Habits of Joy-Filled Marriages*.

Chapter 4: Removing Roadblocks

1. This story was used in a blog I wrote: Chris Coursey, "When the Fuse Is Too Short," THRIVEtoday, June 4, 2019, https://thrive today.org/when-the-fuse-is-too-short/.

2. Learn more with Stephanie Hinman and Marcus Warner, *Building Bounce: How to Grow Emotional Resilience* (Carmel, IN: Deeper Walk International, 2020).

3. Learn more about the Life Model at lifemodelworks.org.

4. James G. Friesen, E. James Wilder, Anne M. Bierling, Rick Koepcke, and Maribeth Poole, *Living from the Heart Jesus Gave You* (East Peoria, IL: Shepherd's House, Inc., 2013), 83–89.

5. These and more can be found in Friesen et al., *Living from the Heart Jesus Gave You*, 85.

6. Learn more with Friesen et al., *Living from the Heart Jesus Gave You*, and Karl Lehman, *Outsmarting Yourself: Catching Your Past Invading the Present and What to Do about It* (Libertyville, IL: This JOY! Books, 2011).

7. Lehman, *Outsmarting Yourself*.

8. Learn more in E. James Wilder, *The Pandora Problem: Facing Narcissism in Leaders & Ourselves* (Carmel, IN: Deeper Walk International, 2018).

9. Learn more with Wilder et al., *Joy Starts Here: The Transformation Zone* (East Peoria, IL: Shepherd's House, Inc., 2013).

10. Dr. Jim Wilder developed this training in 2001 while I tested the exercises. Together we ran the first training in 2002. Visit thrivetoday .org to see the nineteen relational skills.

11. A lot of hands-on practice on appreciation can be found in Brown and Coursey, *Relational Skills in the Bible: A Bible Study Focused on Relationships* (Carmel, IN: Deeper Walk International, 2019).

12. Alex Korb, *The Upward Spiral: Using Neuroscience to Reverse the Course of Depression, One Small Change at a Time* (Oakland, CA: New Harbinger Publications, Inc, 2015). The areas of the brain are the ventromedial and lateral prefrontal cortex, which is part of the Level 4 in the control center.

13. Korb, *The Upward Spiral*.

14. Learn more with the research of Joel Wong, PhD, associate professor at Indiana University and Joshua Brown, PhD, professor at Indiana University.

15. Marcus Warner and Chris Coursey, *The 4 Habits of Joy-Filled Marriages: How 15 Minutes a Day Will Help You Stay in Love* (Chicago: Moody Publishers, 2019).

Chapter 5: How to *Stay* Relational

1. Marcus Warner and E. James Wilder, *RARE Leadership: 4 Uncommon Habits for Increasing Trust, Joy, and Engagement in the People You Lead* (Chicago: Moody Publishers, 2016), 26–27.

2. Learn more about habits, and the fast-track and slow-track processor in Warner and Wilder, *RARE Leadership*, 29–31.

3. Ibid.

4. Ibid.

5. Learn more in Coursey, *Transforming Fellowship*.

6. Dr. Allan Schore teaches regulating high-energy states (joy) to low-energy states (rest) are the best predictors for lifelong mental health. Learn more about the significance of rest in Wilder et al., *Joy Starts Here: The Transformation Zone* (East Peoria, IL: Shepherd's House, Inc., 2013).

7. Learn more with Wilder et al., *Joy Starts Here: The Transformation Zone*.

8. Adrian Ward, Kristen Duke, Ayelet Gneezy, Maarten Bos, "The Effects of Smartphones on Studying," McCombs School of Business, University of Texas at Austin, February 21, 2018, https://research.utexas.edu/showcase/articles/view/the-effects-of-smartphones-on-studying.

9. Ward et al., "The Effects of Smartphones."

10. See more with Larry D. Rosen, "The Distracted Student Mind—Enhancing Its Focus and Attention," *Phi Delta Kapan*, October 1, 2017, https://kappanonline.org/rosen-distracted-student-mind-attention/.

11. Linda Stone, "Are You Breathing? Do You Have Email Apnea?," LindaStone.net, November 24, 2014, https://lindastone.net/tag/screen-apnea/.

12. Stone mentions these were dancers, musicians, an Ironman triathlete (among other high performance athletes), and a test pilot.

13. We are indebted to Dr. Jim Wilder for helping us develop this habit.

14. This exercise is based on the work and writings of Dr. Daniel Siegel at drdansiegel.com.

15. Based on the "Rest and Joy" exercise by Marcus Warner and Chris Coursey, *The 4 Habits of Joy-Filled Marriages: How 15 Minutes a Day Will Help You Stay in Love* (Chicago: Moody Publishers, 2019), 109–10.

Chapter 6: Sustaining the Switched-On Life

1. Learn more with Allan Schore, *The Development of the Unconscious Mind* (New York: W. W. Norton & Company, 2019).

2. Suffering well is a Life Model concept from Thomas Gerlauch used to contrast trauma. Suffering well means we are still relational; we remember who we are while we endure pain. Trauma pushes us into nonrelational mode where we lose ourselves.

3. E. James Wilder, *The Pandora Problem: Facing Narcissism in Leaders & Ourselves* (Carmel, IN: Deeper Walk International, 2018).

4. Learn more about enemy mode in Wilder, *The Pandora Problem*.

5. Shepherd's House, Inc., *Passing the Peace after a Crisis*, vs. 3.1 (East Peoria, IL: Shepherd's House, Inc., 2015), 7.

6. Ed Khouri and Jim Wilder, *Belonging Facilitator Workbook* (Pasadena, CA: Shepherd's House, Inc., 2010), 48.

7. For more on this, read Shepherd's House, Inc., *Passing the Peace*.

8. The work of Dr. Jim Wilder (lifemodelworks.org), Dr. Karl Lehman (immanuelapproach.com), and Ed Khouri (equippinghearts.com) have contributed to these exercises.

9. The Shalom My Body exercises are based on the work of neurotherapist Suzanne Day (neuroclinicbarrie.com) and the work of Dr. Jim Wilder (lifemodelworks.org), Ed Khouri (equippinghearts.com),

and Dr. Karl Lehman (immanuelapproach.com). Watch a demonstration of the Shalom My Body exercises on the Chris Coursey – THRIVEtoday YouTube page at https://www.youtube.com/user /Thrivingtoday.

10. Learn more about this practice with Lehman, *Outsmarting Yourself*, 200ff.

11. Chris Coursey – THRIVEtoday, YouTube page at https://www .youtube.com/user/Thrivingtoday.

12. Chris Coursey – THRIVEtoday, YouTube page at https://www .youtube.com/user/Thrivingtoday and Dr. Jim Wilder demonstrates the exercises in the Year One course in the THRIVE-at-Home series at thrivetoday.org.

13. Stephanie Hinman and Marcus Warner, *Building Bounce: How to Grow Emotional Resilience* (Carmel, IN: Deeper Walk International, 2020).

14. Lehman, *Outsmarting Yourself*, 245.

Chapter 7: Starting a Relational Revival

1. Training through THRIVEtoday events (thrivetoday.org), including the work of Dr. Jim Wilder (lifemodelworks.org), Dr. Karl Lehman (immanuelapproach.com), John and Sungshim Loppnow (presenceandpractice.com), and more colleagues and partner organizations. Visit thrivetoday.org to view resources.

2. Christians believe the prophet Isaiah prophesied Jesus to be the Prince of Peace in Isaiah 9:6, and 1 Corinthians 14:33 refers to God as a God of peace.

3. Reference to Matthew 5:45.

4. Learn more with Michel Hendricks and E. James Wilder, *The Other Half of Church: Christian Community, Brain Science, and Overcoming Spiritual Stagnation* (Chicago: Moody Publishers, 2020).

5. One example is Korah in Psalm 42.

6. A few examples are Psalm 46:1, Matthew 7:7, and Hebrews 4:15–16.

7. Psalm 50:10.

8. Learn more in Karl Lehman, *The Immanuel Approach: For Emotional Healing & for Life* (Evanston, IL: Immanuel Publishing, 2016) and E. James Wilder, Anna Kang, John Loppnow, and Sungshim Lop-

pnow, *Joyful Journey: Listening to Immanuel* (East Peoria, IL: Shepherd's House, Inc., 2015).

9. Learn more about these steps with E. James Wilder and Chris Coursey, *Share Immanuel: The Healing Lifestyle* (East Peoria, IL: Shepherd's House, Inc., 2010).

10. Reference to 2 Corinthians 12:9.

11. This exercise is based on Skill 16 of the 19 skills, *Recognizing High and Low Energy Response Styles*. Learn more about this skill in my book Coursey, *Transforming Fellowship*.

WHAT SEPARATES HAPPY MARRIAGES FROM MISERABLE ONES?

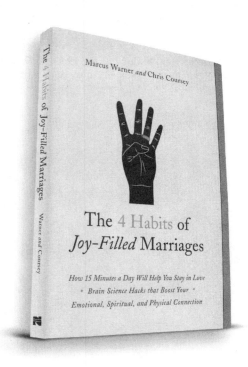

These authors have studied relationships (and neuroscience) and discovered four habits that keep joy regular and problems small. Some couples do them naturally, but anyone can learn. Retrain your brain to make joy your default setting by practicing the field-tested 15-minute exercises at the end of each chapter.

978-0-8024-1907-1 | also available as eBook and audiobook

"Most people spend far more time in preparation for their vocation than they do in preparation for marriage."

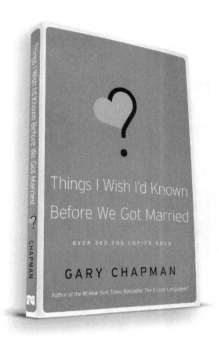

SIMPLE IDEAS, LASTING LOVE.

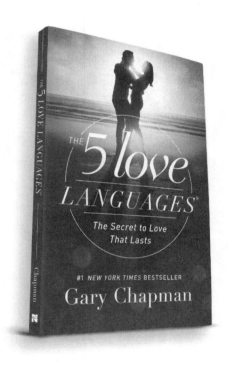

Discover the secret that has transformed millions of relationships worldwide. Whether your relationship is flourishing or failing, Dr. Gary Chapman's proven approach to showing and receiving love will help you experience deeper and richer levels of intimacy with your partner—starting today.

978-0-8024-1270-6 | also available as eBook and audiobook